Social Studies at the Center

Social Studies at the Center

Integrating Kids, Content, and Literacy

Tarry Lindquist
Douglas Selwyn

HEINEMANN
Portsmouth, NH

Heinemann
A division of Reed Elsevier Inc.
361 Hanover Street
Portsmouth, NH 03801–3912
www.heinemann.com

Offices and agents throughout the world

The authors and publisher wish to thank those who have generously given permission to reprint borrowed material:

"Essential Skills for Social Studies" from Appendix A of *Curriculum Standards for Social Studies: Expectations of Excellence*, 1994, Bulletin 89. Reprinted by permission of the National Council for the Social Studies.

Library of Congress Cataloging-in-Publication Data
Lindquist, Tarry.
 Social studies at the center : integrating kids, content, and literacy / Tarry Lindquist, Douglas Selwyn ; [editor, William Varner].
  p. cm.
 Includes bibliographical references.
 ISBN 0-325-00168-5 (alk. paper)
 1. Social sciences—Study and teaching (Elementary)—United States. 2. Social sciences—Study and teaching (Middle school)—United States. I. Selwyn Douglas, 1949– II. Varner, William. III. Title.

LB1584.L543 2000
372.83'044—dc21

                                                    99–047993

Editor: William Varner
Production: Elizabeth Valway
Cover design: Jenny Jensen Greenleaf
Cover and interior photos: Judi Slepyan
Manufacturing: Louise Richardson

Printed in the United States of America on acid-free paper

11 10 09 08 07 VP 8 9 10 11 12

Contents

Foreword

One of the joys of living in three states—first Colorado, then Texas, and, for fifteen years now, Washington—has been getting to know the teachers. There are so many fine teachers—smart, caring, knowledgeable, creative, and deeply reflective. When I hear criticism of "the schools," which is so fashionable today, I jump quickly and—I admit— defensively to their aid.

In cities and suburbs across the country and in rural areas too, teachers are "keepers of the fire." I mean by "fire" a vision of a well-educated public that can meet the challenge of living together democratically in a diverse society. With each new outbreak of "ethnic cleansing" somewhere in the world, with each new "hate crime" committed in our own communities, with each widening of the gap between rich and poor, we are reminded that democracy is a fragile social and political system. Many people in the United States take democracy for granted, but schoolteachers cannot. They are democracy's stewards.

I have known Tarry and Doug, the coauthors of this book, for years. They are keepers of the fire, and they are *master* teachers. I don't mean *master* in the bureaucratic sense, that is, where someone has taught a certain number of years, or supervised a certain number of student teachers, or earned a certain number of advanced degrees, or headed up committees and task forces. Tarry and Doug meet those requirements easily—without getting up in the morning, one could say. I am referring to something else, something resounding: You would give anything for them to teach your children, and you would give anything to retake just one year of your own elementary education, only this time with Tarry or Doug as your teacher.

In lieu of that firsthand experience, you have in your hands their book. They have both written about their teaching before, but separately. Now they join together and present in one volume their social studies–based approach to teaching and curriculum planning in the elementary school.

What is most helpful about the book, in my view, is what is at its core: two richly detailed accounts of units they have planned and taught to fourth- and fifth-grade children. Tarry's Windows on the World unit and Doug's Immigration unit are, as you will see, full-blown, integrated courses of study and experience. Tarry and Doug's basic approach is *to make social studies the organizational hub of the school curriculum and the school day*, integrating and unifying teaching and learning around a single, powerful concept. Why do they do this? There are numerous good reasons, as you are about to read, and among them is a wonderfully practical one: The approach "allows us and our students to integrate the day into a meaningful whole, with the work done in language arts informed by and supporting that which is studied in social studies, science, or art. We can think in one major conceptual direction (rather than six), bringing the various disciplines to that central location."

The litmus test for such an approach is the power, depth, and reach of the social studies concept that is placed at the hub. Does the concept help children enlarge their knowledge and experience *now*, as an immediate consequence of this unit of study? And does it help them learn more *later*, too, by serving as a foundation in the years to come? That is, has a concept that is both *important* and *foundational* been placed at the integrating core of the teacher's and students' day? Such a concept is generative, for it grows with the child while it helps the child grow. A good foundation will support not only a house today but much remodeling and adding on in years to come. A house today, a castle in ten years. Judge for yourself as you read the in-depth descriptions of the two units: How do Windows on the

World and Immigration fare against this criterion? Are generative concepts at their core?

Tarry and Doug hope this book will aid new and experienced teachers alike who may be reluctant to step into new territory where powerful social studies subject matter serves as the organizational and conceptual center of the school curriculum and the school day. I invite you to let this book serve as a wise veteran teacher "down the hall," who can ease us into this sort of ambitious social studies–based work with children.

Walter Parker
Professor of Education
University of Washington, Seattle

Acknowledgments

From Tarry

Thanks to my students, the Class of 2006, for making learning come alive. Thanks to Doug Selwyn for his considerate cooperation and the many hours of thoughtful conversation we shared about this best of professions.

Thanks to my colleagues at Lakeridge Elementary for an atmosphere of unconditional regard.

Thanks to my social studies friends, especially Marj Montgomery, Rick Moulden, Marte Peet, and Oralee Kramer, for their insight and creativity. Thanks to NCSS for the opportunities to explore, to learn, and to serve. Thanks to Meg Bozzone for inviting me into her world at Creative Classroom. Thanks to my daughters, Tia and Tani, for their continued encouragement. Thanks to my mother-in-law, Katharine Lindquist, for her excellent model of how to live a life of graciousness and my granddaughter, Taylor, for her gift of love.

Thanks to my husband, Malcolm, for his never-ending support, help, and humor.

From Tarry and Doug

Thanks to the Heinemann crew for all their assistance and expertise, especially Bill Varner, editor extraordinaire, and Elizabeth Valway, production editor, who shaped us up better than we knew we could be.

From Doug
I'd like to begin by thanking the students in C-1, who are bright, beautiful, and a joy to be with. Thank you Xaviar, Tracy, Kjell, Veronica, Leung, Kathryn, Cassie, Arydai, Delbert, David, Rashonda, Jonathan, Steve, Thanh, LaToya, Kristina, Leimomi, Charly, Kenneth, Cesara, Deno, Ryan, and Cesar. I love that your names cause the spell checker to work overtime. You are the world and this book has you at its heart. Thank you Tarry. I've wanted to work with you for a long time, a cheap excuse to know more of what you know. Well, I still don't know what you know, but I have learned plenty and enjoyed the process immensely.

And Mac. You teach your classes, working daily and weekends, and somehow still have time to take care of the rest of us. Thank you. Kim Norton, my coteacher at Puget Sound Writing Project, offered much support and a careful reading of my first pages. She provided wise and tactful counsel.

Holly Stein and Jack Brenner are the codirectors of the Puget Sound Writing Project and they have an amazing ability to create a space that is at once inspiring, safe, and useful. I have a deep appreciation for the unique and precious gift they offer teachers in the Puget Sound area.

Members of the Beacon Hill staff and community volunteered their time to be interviewed by my students as we gathered data for our "coming to Seattle" stories. Many of them had very difficult stories to tell, and they told them with great gentleness and generosity. Lela Chung, Jo Cripps, and Gail Mitchell are teachers (and friends) who took the time to read early versions of the immigration unit and my planning process. Their careful readings were very helpful in shaping the final version of that chapter. Jo also took time to offer her considerable editing skills for a particularly knotty section of text.

Don Fels, cereal surrealist reminds me constantly that the world is an extraordinarily interesting place, and that we are all interconnected. His perpetual interest in the world is catching, at least a little. It is a powerful and wonderful gift. He also introduced me to the cereal box construction sequence.

Steve Goldenberg is so out of step in these standards-based times that he actually centers his classroom around the students. Stubborn lad, extraordinary teacher.

Thank you Derek Mills, and I hope you have landed gently.

Noah, Josh, and Rachelle (my stepchildren) have lived their lives as profound and unique learners. They are clear evidence that one size does not fit all.

Jan Maher, beloved and friend, is an extraordinary writer and teacher. She continues to amaze, and I am thankful for our lives together.

This book is dedicated first to Judi Slepyan. Judi is an extraordinary photographer; her photographs light up this book. She has an uncanny ability to see people as they truly are, and to communicate that through her pictures. I really see my students in her work, and she knows them so well that it helps them to know themselves better. They continue to look through our notebook of photographs (of the students), fascinated and excited to be given such loving and skillful attention. But Judi's photographs are the smaller half of the story. She is so generous with her time, energies, and resources that she leaves us in awe. She volunteered countless hours to work with my students to teach them the basics of photography and to help them learn to develop their pictures. She has volunteered for so many classrooms and organizations, donating her skills and enthusiasm. It seems to be her lot in life to make what she touches much, much better.

Finally, I'd like to dedicate this book to my parents. They have known each other since childhood and married on my father's way into the army and World War II. They have lived through the staggering changes of this century and have retained their basic values of kindness, civility, integrity, and humor. This book is dedicated to them, with love and appreciation.

Introduction

That, I believe, is what we need to bring to our schools: experiences that are so full of the wonder of life, so full of connectedness, so embedded in the context of our communities, so brilliant in the insights that we develop and the analyses that we devise, that all of us, teachers and students alike, can learn to live lives that leave us truly satisfied. Delpit (104)

View of Teaching and Learning

Social Studies at the Center presents a view of teaching and learning that emphasizes meaning and understanding over coverage and facts. We support an integrated approach to teaching social studies, but more than that, we advocate placing social studies at the center of the entire school curriculum. Social studies as an organizing hub allows for a systematic process of learning. For example, students study the geography, culture, religion, economics, and history of a location that happens to be the setting for a novel, or historical fiction they are reading. Students compare and contrast the people and places they are reading about with their own time and place. They practice bringing together various learning experiences into the realm of usable knowledge. Students are learning how to question, how to organize and evaluate their own experiences, how to connect what they have assimilated, and how to communicate about it. They are, in fact, learning how to learn.

Volume of Content

It is our experience that many schools treat social studies as a problem child. On the one hand, elementary teachers may find ways to not teach the subject because they have little training or interest in it; or they feel they have too little time to develop a comprehensive social studies program, given the other demands on their time and energy. When they do offer social studies, it is often a lesson, adhering to the teaching directions supplied by whatever text has been adopted by their district. On the other hand, upper-grade teachers might be very knowledgeable in their discipline, but they are often appalled and discouraged by the pace at which they must teach. World-history teachers, for example, are often expected to know something about every part of the world. Thus, they lean heavily on the world-history text for at least the first several years of teaching, as they gather information and additional resources about the various places and times they cover in class. The same is true for elementary teachers who are required to teach incredible amounts of information, such as all of U.S. history, Canada, and Mexico in one school year.

Some teachers get lost in content and forget there are specific social studies skills that students need to acquire. Reading a time line, collecting data, comparing information from different points of view, identifying bias, and debating issues from more than one side are just a sample of the kinds of skills these future citizens need.

An Ambiguous Message

Most elementary teachers do not see themselves as social studies teachers. When asked, we tend to respond that we are reading teachers or math teachers; or, most likely, teachers of children. Social studies education at most training programs for teachers is minimal. Many teachers receive little education regarding social studies content and what content we do get is often provided on a narrow disciplinary basis: economics, history, sociology, geography, and so forth . . . No wonder our "mission to teach social studies" is hazy.

Additionally, school districts and legislatures often send elementary- and middle-school teachers a clear message: teach reading, teach math, teach writing. Frequently, there is no mention of social studies. Many of the states that have inaugurated statewide standards are rigorous in their assessment of reading, writing, and mathematical skills. Not so with social studies!

Some of the confusion regarding social studies is due to the fact that social studies is a combination of many disciplines such as history, economics, civics, and political science; few education leaders agree on which ones kids need most. Social studies also is a ticklish subject politically because of its very nature.

> The primary purpose of social studies is to help young people develop the ability to make informed and reasoned decisions for the public good as citizens of a culturally diverse, democratic society in an interdependent world. (*Curriculum Standards for Social Studies: Expectations of Excellence*, 1994, vii)

Law makers and educational-policy pundits understand that students who are informed and who do make reasoned decisions may also question traditional values and behaviors, which does not always bode well with certain constituencies. Hence, social studies reform from the state level tends to be meager compared to reform for reading, writing, and math.

Perhaps that's just as well. Social studies reform is occurring from a "bubble up" image rather than the "trickle down" model. Educators, not politicians and businesspeople, are leading the way in social studies reform. Classroom teachers, college researchers, and teacher trainers across the country are examining social studies practices and determining better ways to teach and reach students, pre-K through adult.

> Social studies is the integrated study of the social sciences and humanities to promote civic competence. Within the school program, social studies provides coordinated, systematic study

drawing upon such disciplines as anthropology, archaeology, economics, geography, history, law, philosophy, political science, psychology, religion, and sociology, as well as appropriate content from the humanities, mathematics, and natural sciences. The primary purpose of social studies is to help young people develop the ability to make informed and reasoned decisions for the public good as citizens of a culturally diverse, democratic society in an interdependent world. (*Curriculum Standards for Social Studies: Expectations of Excellence*, 1994, vii)

Enormous Discipline

Social studies is an enormous discipline. Just look at the definition of social studies above. For this reason, it is essential that we learn to plan in ways that will enable our classes to learn efficiently. It is not possible to teach everything that has ever happened, so it becomes of paramount importance for us to identify themes and concepts that allow the students to at least begin to understand how to learn about the world. Teachers can organize lessons so the students will gain skills in planning and carrying out research, in working with a variety of research media, and in communicating about what they have learned. We can develop strategies for helping our students to become literate in "reading the world," and in finding their ways into knowledge.

Social Studies Textbooks

Up until recently, the social studies textbook has been the curriculum. Teachers are frequently set up in their classrooms with little to guide them except the textbook and, perhaps, a vague syllabus that may consist of one word, such as *communities* or *Native Americans*; or an overwhelming list of requirements. Some schools or districts offer more specific guidance about what is expected in the social studies classroom (or social studies portions of the elementary classroom), but it varies greatly. The real guidance often comes from a veteran teacher down the hall or from an educational leader in the school who spells out some specifics about what to teach, who offers to loan materials, and shares ideas and conversation about how he or she approaches the work of social studies.

Point of View

Point of view is one of the most crucial skills that social studies can offer students. Consider this scene from almost any elementary school. A student comes in from the playground, in tears. She tells the story of how she was hit by another student in the class while they were playing a game of kickball. She did nothing to provoke the attack; the other student just hit her. You are about to go looking for the alleged offender when he enters the room, also in tears. His story, between sobs, is that the girl stole the ball so that she and her friends could play kickball, and they wouldn't let him play. Then, when he started to cry, they laughed at him; so he hit her. The situation is now a bit more complicated, and gets still more so when a few witnesses arrive to offer their versions of events. It is likely (or at least possible) that none of the students is consciously lying, but the stories reflect different points of view. It's a little like the social studies, which is the study of real life.

Social studies must clearly communicate that point of view is an essential element of any story. Who is telling the story (about Columbus, Bunker Hill, Hiroshima, smart bombs, the Bay of Pigs, the three little pigs) and their relationship to the story, is important to know. Whose voices we are *not* hearing are as important as the voices we *are* hearing.

Students can practice point of view quite effectively and practice language-arts skills at the same time. Consider assigning the kids the task of writing a letter, as if they were Pocahontas or John Smith. Try having them keep a journal as they read a historical-fiction novel, as if they were the main character. Do point-of-view newspapers. For example, after studying the Civil War, have the kids create three different front pages of a newspaper: one from the northern point of view, one from the southern, and one from a free-black point of view.

Abraham Lincoln's voice	Both Voices	Jefferson Davis' voice
Four score and seven years ago . . .		
		I read a book by Harriet Beecher Stowe . . .
It changed my life		
		And that of the country, too. Now I am Gray.
And I am Blue.		
	For years we've fought	
		But no one thought
It would lead to our families being shot		
	For years we've fought	
		Whether hand-to-hand
Or with drummer boys in a band		
	This is called the Civil War And it was liberty We were fighting for.	

This poem for two voices is written from two points of view by Andie and Sydney after studying the Civil War in fifth grade.

Multiple points of view do not begin with a textbook. Multiple points of view begin with the very structure of our classrooms. In fact, encouraging multiple points of view is the keystone of a democratic classroom. Modeling how multiple points of view are valued in our classrooms is powerful. Strategies that provoke different points of view help kids practice expressing their convictions and listening to others. Providing opportunities for students to give their opinion, whether it's during social studies, reading, or math, reinforces that many points of view are not only okay, but desirable.

A rich curriculum, an integrated curriculum, frees our classrooms from perpetuating a single dominant cultural heritage. More than ever we are obligated to find more than one side of the story, to look at the way people live from many sides, and to elicit minority opinions. Similarly, we need to encourage students to weigh the costs and benefits of decisions, to examine both the benefactor and the recipient, to perceive the hidden agenda and to question the validity of one-sided or simplistic arguments.

Fitting All the Subjects In

Integrating a curriculum centered on a social studies theme allows a teacher to meet multiple curricular needs. A unit centered on a topic such as homelessness, or space travel, change, conflict, neighborhoods, or immigration allows the teacher to organize a curriculum that encompasses the reading/writing/grammar areas of curriculum. The students are reading and writing about their neighborhoods, pioneering the American West, or immigrating to a new country. There are ample opportunities to write in many different modes (expository, fiction, poetry, persuasive, editorial, report, journal, newspaper-style). There are often science aspects to the topics, ranging from weather, plants, and vegetation, to more complex cases such as pollution and air quality, water quality, the survival of salmon, buffalo, green belts, and ecosystems. It is hard to imagine a teacher having time to teach without integrating the curriculum, and social studies serves as the perfect center to such integration, dealing as it does with all aspects of our lives.

Integrated Curriculum

Organizing instruction into broad, thematically based clusters of work through which reading, writing, and speaking activities are interrelated promotes understanding of the connections among activities and ideas. This is what we call an integrated curriculum. In the last ten years, research demonstrating the power of such approaches has begun to appear, first with early language development, more recently, with respect to teaching in the upper grades. We have found activities designed around a unifying concept build on each other, rather than remaining as fragmented disciplines. We've discovered that perhaps it is not necessary to have a social studies period, a reading period, a language-arts period, separate and isolated each day. In fact, we advocate wrapping the disciplines together. Creating a connection of ideas as well as of related skills provides opportunities for reinforcement. Additionally, sharp divisions among disciplines often creates duplication of skills that is seldom generalized by our students. However, as the authors of *Best Practices, Second Edition* note, when concepts are developed over a period of time so that one day's reading prepares students for the next day's discussion, writing, and decision making, young people are more likely to grasp the connections among ideas and to develop and understand broad generalizations (184–188).

Life Is Easier

Integrating the curriculum can make life much easier for teachers and students. Most elementary-classroom teachers teach all the subjects to one group of students throughout the day (recognizing there are students who may be pulled out for various reasons throughout). This arrangement makes it possible to integrate much or all of the day's curriculum so that it all fits together logically, thematically, and through content—each piece reinforcing what is covered throughout the day. For example, if the class is studying space travel, students can read stories about space, write letters defending (or challenging) the space program, send postcards from the planets describing what is seen from the surface, or write poems about the moon. All the while, they practice proper format, persuasive writing, or sentence elaboration. Students can study flight and the properties that support life on earth in science. They can measure the shape and size of the various planets, plot the distance and times for travel from one planet to another, and calculate relative weights on the different planets as part of their math study.

A colony on a new planet would need to develop the basic building blocks of any society. These would likely include creating a government, a governing document, defining jobs, mapping the terrain, dealing with any native populations encountered, and providing for the well being of the travelers (food, water, shelter, safety). All of these issues are the stuff of social studies.

Students can create art pieces that fit in with the space mission, such as mobiles of the solar system, maps of the various planets, insignias for the spacecraft and uniforms, and the uniforms themselves. They can design the structures that will keep astronauts from earth safe on the various planets they explore. They can create various life forms that appear on other planets, informed by the conditions unique to those sites.

There is hardly any topic that will not fit into the larger integrative approach of space travel, and that theme is one of dozens that can serve as the hub or centerpiece of a coordinated system of study.

Customized Learning

Imagine classrooms where learning is customized to the children, the conditions, and the criteria or standards that are being met. Picture a place where one size does not fit all, where teachers think of themselves as curriculum designers, not as rubber stamps of teacher's manuals. Certainly, teachers may take a pattern or an idea from a textbook, borrow an activity from the displays down the hall, or try out a simulation learned at a workshop, but they know they have choices to make to shape lessons and units to fit their own classes, and personalize learning with strategies their own kids need to practice and apply. Teachers deliberately plan units that integrate knowledge, skills, and attitudes around a central theme or concept because they know that what they are constructing helps kids learn better. Instead of isolated lessons that lead to nowhere, the students in these classrooms can identify where they've been, where they are going, and how all they have learned in between connects.

Take a Trip

Think of a unit plan as a trip. Know where you are. Know where you're going. As a beginning teacher or someone new to a grade level, you may decide to take the shortest distance between two points. Determine what it is the children need to know, need to do, and need to feel to get from point A to point B. But you don't need to travel steerage. Upgrade the trip by pulling in language arts, the arts, and social-participation skills. These additions will make the trip more pleasant and more successful.

Each year you teach the unit, you'll be able to add new destinations or plan a different route to get where you want to go. These plans may be influenced by recent district or state adoptions and assessments, new knowledge you have gained regarding the topic, student input and interest, or new materials and resources you have discovered.

Like a traveler, you have a budget. In most of our classrooms the budget is not currency, but time. How much time does it take to teach this unit? Some years teachers find they are able to take more time than others. Some years the students work more efficiently than others. Sometimes we connect the destination with the starting point as quickly as possible. Other times we have the leisure to meander, building up experiential knowledge and skills.

Practical Benefits

One benefit of placing social studies at the center of the curriculum is the teacher and the students have more control of their day. When content connects, when activities blend and extend learning, children work with purpose and joy. Discipline more often comes from within each student as personal goals are challenged. The kids don't get bored because they are involved in the pursuit of knowledge that matters. Learning makes sense. Projects are given the time needed. This doesn't mean that students do the same thing all day. Far from it. Another benefit is one of time. Instead of staying at school until 7:00 P.M. trying to figure out what to do for the next day, you'll find that each day's purpose is clear.

Integration calls upon the teacher to orchestrate the day. Like a symphony, school days need not be conducted at one tempo or be played by only the string section. Integration makes it possible for us to arrange the day's activities so there are working times and talking times, buddy times and alone times, kinesthetic times and reflective times.

Doug and Tarry: Two Voices

We have organized this book to assist teachers who are interested in moving away from the traditional textbook but are not sure how to do that, either because they are new to the profession, or because they are interested in broadening their approach to teaching. You will notice two voices throughout this book, Doug's and Tarry's. We teach in different schools: one urban and one suburban. We come to teaching with different backgrounds and experiences. However, we both believe in integrated units, small-group work, hands-on projects, kid-centered research, assessment that makes a difference, and reflections that call upon our students to use their heads and their hearts. While we both share many of the same goals in terms of what we think is important in our social studies-centered classrooms, we have different ways of getting there. This book demonstrates some of the many ways to teach social studies. We have created templates for constructing integrated unit plans based around a core theme or concept to help those teachers who'd like to try a more connected kind of learning in their classrooms. Two examples of units that we teach, developed according to the templates and using a variety of teaching and learning strategies with commentary about those units, are provided with the notion that they can be used as models for other topics. There is a chapter devoted to questions we have been asked frequently, at workshops or by teachers in schools, and hopefully some of yours are included. Finally, we offer resources that will support a social studies program that is neither defined by, nor limited to, the assigned textbook.

FIGURE I–1 *It Takes a Group to Make a World*

Moving to the Center

Social Studies at the Center is written to help each teacher make effective choices and to encourage everyone to create a social studies program that unifies and integrates the teaching day. We think this book will help teachers plan units so that students can learn how to study topics in depth, to question and research efficiently, and to experience the excitement and joy of finding out about who they are and how they came to be this way. It is our experience that teachers who move social studies to the center of their curriculum find their days more connected and coordinated.

A Way of Looking at the World

Social Studies at the Center is as much about ways of looking at the world as it is a book specifically about the teaching of social studies, and it presents a definite point of view. There are discrete disciplines in a school curriculum and things to learn from each, but the learning is most long lasting and valuable if the students can make sense of it in an integrated, real-world context. We want students to know things and to know how to think about the things they know in ways that help them to "see the whole."

We want this book to serve as the veteran teacher down the hall, a mentor. *Social Studies at the Center* will be that educational leader who not only provides basic, essential information about teaching social studies but also nudges the new or uncertain teacher toward educationally sound choices and excellent teaching practices. In addition to providing a large repertoire of learning strategies, this book will demonstrate how intermediate and middle-school teachers can place social studies content, skills, and knowledge at the center of their school day and reap a benefit that reaches way beyond the social studies period. In our classrooms, we've found student success across the curriculum increases. Student motivation and interest rises. The need for student discipline decreases. This book will also appeal to dedicated social studies teachers, affirming what they already are doing, reminding them of things they used to do, and providing them with new strategies and insights into their own teaching.

An Annotated Table of Contents

plagiarizing. It also demonstrates how deliberate planning can capitalize on the knowledge and skills practiced in one unit for the foundation of extended, more demanding study in a subsequent unit. A template is provided.

Chapter 3: Doug's Unit: Immigration
Doug designed this unit to mine the resources of the students in his inner-city classroom. He takes advantage of his students' family histories to explore the concept of immigration and what it has meant to people moving from one place to another. This unit models how learning, all day long, can be student centered as well as social studies centered. A template is provided.

Chapter 4: Questions and Responses
These are the questions that teachers often want to ask but don't. Why? Sometimes they feel they have no one to ask. Sometimes they are too embarrassed to admit they don't know the answers. This chapter of the book is dedicated to responding to both common and uncommon questions by teachers about the teaching and learning of social studies. School supervisors and administrators will find this chapter equally beneficial as they provide support for their teachers in reaching new levels of success in social studies.

Chapter 5: Our Favorite Strategies, Resources, and Websites
Wrapping up the book, we share sixty-eight practical, integrative strategies for teachers who are interested in organizing their curriculum around a social studies center. We also pooled the resources and websites we use most to help teachers strengthen their own social studies classrooms. A brief review of national social studies standards and a list of possible assessment strategies that

facilitate moving social studies to the center are included as well.

Appendix: The Essential Social Studies Skills
The Essential Social Studies Skills Checklist
Window on the World Checklist
Immigrant Biography
The Model House Project
Housing Project
Reflection on Model Project

Chapter Bibliography

DELPIT, LISA. 1995. *Other People's Children*. New York: New Press.

National Council for the Social Studies. 1994. *Curriculum Standards for Social Studies: Expectations of Excellence*. Washington, D.C.: National Council for the Social Studies.

ZEMELMAN, STEVEN, HARVEY DANIELS, and ARTHUR HYDE. 1998. *Best Practice: New Standards for Teaching and Learning in America's Schools*, 2nd ed. Portsmouth, NH: Heinemann.

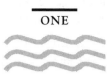

ONE

Integrated Curriculum

An integrated curriculum is at the heart of a teaching approach that places social studies at the center of the curriculum. Social studies becomes the hub, the center of the wheel that is a seamless, coherent course of study that extends throughout the school day. Whatever the students do at the start of school will be reinforced and extended throughout the day. Discrete skills related to the various subjects and disciplines are still taught, but there is a consistent thread of content and context that keeps the learning focused. Ackerman and Perkins write, "In its broadest sense curriculum integration embraces not just the interweaving of subjects (e.g., science and social studies) but of any curriculum elements (e.g., skills and content) that might be taught more effectively in relation to each other than separately" (Ackerman and Perkins, in Jacobs 1989, 79).

In our classrooms language arts, reading, writing, listening, speaking, and thinking are most often and most easily linked to social studies content. Look at the essential social studies skills in the appendix and you'll see they are often one and the same. Some concepts connect science and social studies quite effortlessly, especially those that explore issues and concerns in today's world. As Anderson and his colleagues noted in *Becoming a Nation of Readers*, "The most logical place for most reading and thinking strategies is in the social studies and sciences rather than in separate lessons about reading" (Anderson et al. 1985, 73). Environmental issues such as global warming, endangered species, and the quality of the air and water lend themselves to multidisciplinary, integrated study, as do explorations of inventions and technological change that have affected both people and environments.

For us, math integrates into social studies content when students are called upon to apply logical/mathematical-oriented skills, such as classifying and organizing data, statistics and probability, diagrams, and time lines. We do not invent artificial math or science connections just for the sake of "rounding off" a unit. Math, science, and health integrate naturally or not at all, depending on the focus of the unit, the interests of the children, and the skills that need to be introduced and practiced.

Defining the Term

Integrated curriculum is a term that has multiple meanings, and we are using the term broadly, to include as many of those meanings as possible.

1. *Common theme or concept:* We offer units that are integrated in that they focus on a central theme or concept; immigration and "windows on the world." We bring that central concept to each part of the day, be it language arts, science, reading, art, or music, and make use of the common content to explore the various disciplines, even as those disciplines give us a different look at the central concept.

2. *Coordinated classes:* We also integrate in how we coordinate a variety of classes with a common time period or theme. This is relatively easy in most elementary-school situations because we teach almost all the subjects. It is possible to coordinate various classes at the middle- and high-school levels, but it does take more intentional coordination among the various teachers. There is every reason to study the French Revolution in world history, literature of the French Revolution in either French class or language arts, perform Marat Sade in language arts or drama class, and so forth. This is not to minimize the challenges to doing this

kind of planning; each discipline has its own skills and content, and each teacher his or her favorite units. But it can be done, and the rewards are many.

3. *Links:* Another way that we integrate curriculum is by using the methodology of one discipline to study in another. The techniques and methodologies of the arts, for example, can help us to learn more about the social studies, and vice versa. Students are learning about immigration issues through photography, music, art, writing and literature, and science even as they are learning the skills and content of those other disciplines.

4. *Child centered:* Perhaps the most important way in which we strive to integrate our classrooms and curriculum is to draw the lives of our students into the center of what we do. We organize our work to integrate the classroom content and the lives of our students so that they recognize the relevance of the content, and so that they can bring their experiences and interests to the learning. In *Making Integrated Curriculum Work*, Elizabeth Pate, Elaine Homestead, and Karen L. McGinnis agree, "Curriculum integration and motivation go hand in hand. Integrated curriculum provides experiences for students that are inherently compelling. Because students are engaged in meaningful learning stemming from their own interests and concerns, there is an intrinsic motivation to learn. Learning comes from within, from the desire to satisfy curiosities and know more about self and society. The process of learning then becomes as important as what is being learned" (Pate et al. 1997, 8).

5. *K–12 articulation/coordination:* Ideally we would be integrating the learning of students over the course of their K–12 education. We cannot control this within our own classrooms, but we seek to coordinate with others within our schools and district so that students are experiencing a thoughtful, intentional, and well coordinated K–12 education.

6. *Unifying within the discipline:* Our approach also incorporates the full range of the social studies in an integrated manner, rather than a separation or splintering of the social studies disciplines.

FIGURE 1–1 *Betsy and Peter Begin a New Project*

Students cannot understand the economics of a culture or society, for example, without also understanding the history, geography, social organization, institutions, politics, and "neighborhood" of that society. The meaning is only found when the many puzzle pieces are brought together.

Teenage Mutant Ninja Turtles

One year when Doug was teaching third graders, the Teenage Mutant Ninja Turtles were the "in thing." The characters appeared on t-shirts, lunch boxes, pencil cases, notebooks, pajamas, and almost every piece of work his students submitted. These pizza-gobbling sewer dwellers had captured the fancy of the eight- and nine-year old-crowd. Their names—Michelangelo, Leonardo, Raphael, and Donatello—were unknown to the students in any other context. So Doug decided to have his class study the Italian Renaissance and the nature of creativity, starting with some guiding questions:

Who were the namesakes of the Turtles?

What was the Renaissance?

How do people create and invent things?

What did the turtles have in common with these artists (besides their names)?

What can we do in the classroom to be creative?

Doug recalls,

Working with a parent volunteer we introduced the students to the artists for whom the turtles were named, and to their art. We studied their paintings and sculpture, and inventions. We created our own paintings and sculptures. We enacted our own version of the Sistine ceiling, painting the undersides of our desks (on paper taped there). When the students complained of getting tired I urged them on. I turned the lights out and they complained about the dark. I reminded them there were no electric lights in the sixteenth century and told them that Michelangelo had strapped candles to his forehead so he could continue. (We didn't do that.)

Students studied inventions of others and then created their own, everything from pens that actually did homework to carrying cases for homeless men and women on the streets.

The students were excited and interested, immersed as they were in their heroes. We closed the unit by taking a trip to a local museum featuring the work of Leonardo da Vinci. The museum had artwork on the ceiling. One of the students (who spent the early part of the year very reluctant and distant) looked up and literally jumped up and down in his excitement, "Hey, it's just like what we did!"

Levels of Integration

Teaching in an integrated manner is something that, for both of us, developed over time. We each tried to make a few connections among different aspects of the curriculum when we started, but the bulk of our planning was in separate subject areas. We have moved to more comprehensive, integrated planning as we have become more experienced and knowledgeable about the curriculum, and more comfortable in including student strengths, interests, and learning needs in our planning process.

Tarry has written about levels of integration in her first book, *Seeing the Whole Through Social Studies*. She notes that there are different levels of integration, from finding some basic connections across curriculum through organizing the entire day around the marriage of curriculum and students. Doug's own experience and his work with first-year teachers (as a mentor teacher) convince him that it is a rare teacher who can immediately move into a fully integrated program. Most of us need to move more slowly, looking for possible points of connection, or opportunities to compare and contrast (two different forms of government or two different examples of colonization, for example). We might identify a story or novel that takes place in a society the class is studying in social studies. Or we might deliberately plan to teach reading and writing skills through social studies content. As the authors of *Enhancing Social Studies Through Literacy Strategies* note, "Social studies lends itself quite naturally to enhancing the literary ability of students" (Irvin, et al. 1995, 17). The larger steps come with time, with familiarity with curriculum and the students, and a comfort with thinking in larger chunks.

There may also be times when fully integrating the curriculum is inappropriate, considering the various factors of your situation (course content, students, time of year, and so forth). Integration of curriculum is not the end goal; a successful educational experience for you and your students is the bottom line. Use critical judgment when deciding about the level of integration that will be most appropriate for you and your students.

Connections

Working with a concept or theme as a central organizer allows students and teachers to look for connections among specific examples, which leads to a broader, deeper understanding of the subject matter. We are using the terms *concept* and *theme* somewhat interchangeably. There seem to be several different definitions for each term in the literature, and what one author calls a concept another calls a theme. If we see any difference, it may be that a theme is an extended unit of study (over time) centered on a concept. Practically speaking, we are using both terms to refer to the center of the integrated unit of study.

The conceptual center is as much a reflection of an attitude toward a topic as it is the topic itself. This is a crucial point in that it frees the teacher from worrying about whether something is a concept or not. The key is that it allows us to make comparisons, to understand the many aspects that make up the category, and to emphasize its connections and interconnections with the world. A conceptual approach has knowledge as its goal; the gathering of information is in service of higher-level analysis and synthesis.

Concepts

A concept names a category of items, and can refer to either physical or abstract things. Country, village, leadership, scarcity, presidents, transportation, power, religion, food, and work are all examples of concepts. These items are not specific to a particular time, place, or person, and allow the students to compare and contrast among specific examples. Units centered on concepts encourage higher-level thinking because they lead students to develop understanding from various specific examples from within the concept. They emphasize connections, linkages, and an exploration of how things are related. Harmin observes, "We can center a unit around a big idea, such as a concept or generalization. With this strategy we use facts and details to illuminate the big ideas or general skills. As a result, many students remember the facts. They pick them up in passing, much as we learn the names of the streets in our neighborhood by passing them repeatedly" (Harmin 1994, 171).

A class could base a unit of study on the concept "work." Students might identify guiding questions about work such as:

What is work?

What kinds of work are there?

What kinds of work do we do today as compared to fifty or one hundred years ago?

How are the various forms of work similar, and how are they different?

What is the relationship between the geography of a place and the kinds of work that people do?

What are the differences between men's work and women's work in various cultures?

Why are there these differences? Have things changed in recent years? Are there reasons why they should or should not change?

How do societies decide what kinds of work need to be done?

What are different ways that decisions get made about how to do jobs?

How are people trained to do work (or how do they gather the skills and knowledge they need to do their work)?

When do people start working and when do they retire?

Should there be laws about who can work and how much they should be paid?

The potential list of guiding questions is nearly endless, and it becomes evident that this conceptual center encourages questions aimed at large understandings. The class would study specific examples of the central concept of work in order to answer those questions. Students could look at specific examples of different forms of work to see what they have in common. They could identify the various types of work that is done in their own classroom, and could learn what they can about the work that is done in their school. The emphasis in this approach is on understanding the concept as fully as possible through exploration of various specific examples that allow for analysis and synthesis of information. Facts are learned in service of higher-level thinking and analysis.

Specific people, places, or things are examples that fall within or under a concept; they are not concepts themselves. Bill Clinton, France, and grapefruits are specific examples from within a few of the conceptual categories listed above. A unit centered on Bill Clinton might lead to more information about his childhood, his entry into politics, his terms in office, and perhaps his place in history. Because of the focus on him, it would be less likely to shed much light on the nature of leadership, or on helping students to understand how various forms of leadership are similar and different.

Good Sense

Concept-based, integrated teaching allows for a focused, intentional examination of topics from a multifaceted, complex attitude. There are several reasons why this approach to teaching makes good sense:

1. The right concept gives the work of the classroom a focus and provides a guide for making decisions about what to teach.
2. Students understand why they are doing what they are doing because there is coherence to the curriculum.
3. Concept-centered teaching promotes transfer of learning from one context to another.
4. There is a clear link between process and content.
5. Concept-centered teaching can promote learning in context.
6. A topic presented from many different angles/perspectives enables students to acquire a more integrated knowledge base.
7. A concept-based unit encourages both breadth and depth of learning. It emphasizes connections and interconnections, leading students to move toward a unifying understanding that links the specific examples within a thematic strand.

8. Concept-based teaching promotes reflection about what is studied. There is more time to reflect, and students become more explicitly aware of what they are learning and what they need to know.

Things to Consider

Integrated teaching is unlike the more traditional, discipline-based approaches and there are some things to consider when teaching to a central concept:

1. Start-up time can be significant, especially when planning a unit for the first time. Take a small step into planning by picking a relatively narrow area of your curriculum as a first try. Look for links among two or more specific situations that appear similar (two examples of democracies, for example, or two civilizations that developed near rivers), and help your students to explore for similarities and differences.

2. The most effective concepts are ones that are coherent, make real connections to material, provide depth and breadth of learning, and provide for effective use of time. They guide students toward powerful ideas, lead to depth of understanding, and promote the ability and inclination of students to link knowledge and ideas across contexts.

3. Focus on the central concept rather than on isolated activities. Sometimes activities can actually distract students away from goals and outcomes. Students can have a wonderful time with an activity and learn virtually nothing from it that relates to the unit theme.

4. Concept-based teaching is not just another way of saying project-based teaching. There are a full range of teaching strategies and approaches required within a unit. Direct instruction can have a place here, as can worksheets, reading for information, map work, and other, traditional-seeming activities. The major difference is that the learning is connected, and that the learning is centered on understanding a significant concept. Projects are

often central, organizing learning activities within a unit that cause students to bring skills and content learning together, but there is still explicit instruction where needed. Your task as a teacher is to make sure your students know enough to get to higher-level/higher-order thinking about your central concept. "Integrated curriculum attempts should not be seen as an interesting diversion but as a more effective means of presenting the curriculum, whether you wish to teach Plato or feminist literature. The curriculum becomes more relevant when there are connections between subjects rather than strict isolation" (Jacobs 1989. 5).

A Note on the Units to Follow

We offer two versions of integrated curriculum in the next chapters. Our experiences and teaching situations are different, and our approaches to integrating and organizing curriculum are different. We offer them as examples in hopes that they will inspire and encourage you to begin to develop your own approach, one that is consistent with your specific teaching situation and your personal educational philosophy.

Please notice that Doug's immigration unit is presented before his planning process is described, the finished house before the blueprint as our editor, Bill Varner, says. Doug hopes that reading the unit description first will help to provide a context for understanding his planning process. Tarry's presentation is the reverse; she presents her unit-planning process and then her unit in the hope that you will be able to appreciate the unit as a logical consequence of the planning process she describes.

Chapter Bibliography

ANDERSON, RICHARD C., ELFRIEDA H. HIEBERT, JUDITH A. SCOTT, and IAN A.G. WILKINSON. 1985. *Becoming a Nation of Readers: The Report of the Commission on Reading.* Urbana, IL: The Center for the Study of Reading.

Ayres, William, and Patricia Ford, eds. 1996. *City Kids, City Teachers*. New York: New Press.

Harmin, Merrill. 1994. *Inspiring Active Learning: A Handbook for Teachers*. Alexandria, VA: ASCD.

Irvin, Judith L., John P. Lunstrum, Carol Lynch-Brown, and Mary Friend Shepard. 1995. *Enhancing Social Studies Through Literacy Strategies*. Washington, D.C.: NCSS Bulletin 91.

Jacobs, Heidi Hayes (Ed). 1989. *Interdisciplinary Curriculum: Design and Implementation*. Alexandria, VA: ASCD.

Pate, Elizabeth P., Elaine Homestead, and Karen L. McGinnis. 1997. *Making Integrated Curriculum Work*. New York: Teachers College Press.

Parker, Walter, and John Jarolimek. 1997. *Social Studies in Elementary Education*, 10th ed. Upper Saddle River, NJ: Prentice-Hall.

Zemelman, Steven, Harvey Daniels, and Arthur Hyde. 1998. *Best Practice: New Standards for Teaching and Learning in America's Schools*, 2nd ed. Portsmouth, NH: Heinemann.

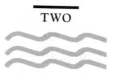

TWO

Tarry's Unit:
Windows on the World

It wasn't until I finally sat down to plan a new social studies unit for my combination class of fourth and fifth graders that I began to panic. World geography! I'd never taught it before. Needless to say, I was uneasy. This was going to take some thought.

Wouldn't it be wonderful, if, in addition to learning geography, I could give my students a "window" on the world? A window where they could gain insights about this earth of ours—not only the geographic regions, the continents, and the countries, but the people who live in them as well. And wouldn't it be even better if my students could look critically at vital problems confronting the world today including environmental and political issues within this topic?

Beginning

Usually I begin organizing a new unit of study by reading. I often start with the social studies text and scan the encyclopedia, reading for basic information, getting a general overview and picking up vocabulary, places, names, and events. Then I deepen my own personal knowledge more quickly by moving to more diverse and specialized books. Actually, I've found using the children's books from our school library worthwhile. Scanning an index, looking for key words and reading selected sections helps me develop a bigger picture of the topic than our social studies teacher's guide provides. This personal research period also points out different ways our study can be organized. I get a sense of the materials readily available to my students. A stop at the public library, browsing through a local bookstore, and an evening on the Internet all inform the choices I have to make about how best to teach this unit to this group of students. It's reassuring to realize that there is no one right way, but a host of ways from which to pick and choose.

Windows on the World?

How can I start a unit that allows my students to construct their own meaning yet get the job done? There are certain concepts and skills my district expects students to know as a result of our study of world geography. Also, there are organizational and management strategies that I want my students to apply as they acquire and use information. As we move academically around the world, there are emotional connections I want to foster, for cultures different from our own: positive, appreciative, and inquisitive. What I really want to do is to give my students a view from which they can sample the world, explore its diverse geography, investigate its different cultures, and create a collection of meaningful information from which they can construct a few generalizations. And we need to accomplish all of this in about three months.

Organization and time management are real issues. In addition to teaching this unit, I have many other lessons to teach in my self-contained, four–five split classroom. Looking for natural connections with other disciplines, I try to anticipate where I might create opportunities to extend the sphere of our study topic. In other words, I am always alert to those places where I can teach a language-arts skill or reinforce a science concept through social studies content.

For me, social studies often anchors my day. In reading, for example, what we read is related to the social studies theme. It may be fiction or nonfiction. What we write, both purpose and content, is connected to the social studies concept. Nearly everything we do informs, enhances, or extends our comprehension of social studies and our capacity to learn.

FIGURE 2–1 *Maryn Cuts and Creates a WOW!*

The real question often centers on how to manage any unit of study in a reasonable way, both for the children and for the teacher. The theme, Windows on the World, kept coming back to me. What did I have available to symbolize a window? And how could I guide my kids to carry out individual research, keep their research in an organized fashion, and present what they have learned in an organized, engaging way? Kids like things that look good. If their product looks too lopsided, ill planned, messy, or unorganized, they will throw it away . . . and the learning involved gets tossed too. All we had on hand was traditional construction paper. However, I knew my kids wouldn't be satisfied with a flat, inert piece of paper. They are a kinesthetic bunch and prefer papers that wiggle, jiggle, or jump.

A couple of kids hung around after school one afternoon, so I asked them to help me create a window. Lots of laughter and several sheets of paper later, we constructed what looked like a reasonable model: two sheets of 12" × 18" construction paper, stapled together on the 12-inch sides, with the top sheet cut down the middle. Looking more like French doors, our paper windows just waited to reveal the interior landscape of some far-off place.

Template

Planning is the crux to good social studies teaching. Knowing where you want to go and ending up there is a reasonable goal. While serendipity is magical and impulse is exciting, constructing a coordinated, articulated, complete social studies program takes planning. It is in the planning that attention is given to the multiple ways children learn. Planning moves integration from the accidental to the intentional. Planning deliberately incorporates new skills, promotes application of learned skills, and encourages desired attitudes. Planning also facilitates moving social studies to the center of the school day as teachers consciously seek those connections where skills and content cross curriculum to benefit students. For example, students who need to practice comparison/contrast paragraphs might compare life in the big house to life in the quarters as part of their pre-Civil War study. Students can be encouraged to apply their understanding of photosynthesis as they discuss the reasons native peoples around the globe tell stories about the sun.

A template or pattern is often helpful when starting something new. For many teachers, moving social studies to the center of the school day is new. Look over the formal template that follows. Then study the working template I used to plan the Windows on the World unit. This graphic organizer, the curriculum disk, may be helpful to you. It helps me. Certainly, like all templates or patterns, this one can be changed to fit the your own needs and resources. Some teachers like to use it initially, as they begin to plan their units, to make sure all the components of a successful (meaning useful, efficient, worthwhile, and fun) unit are accounted for. Others refer to it when

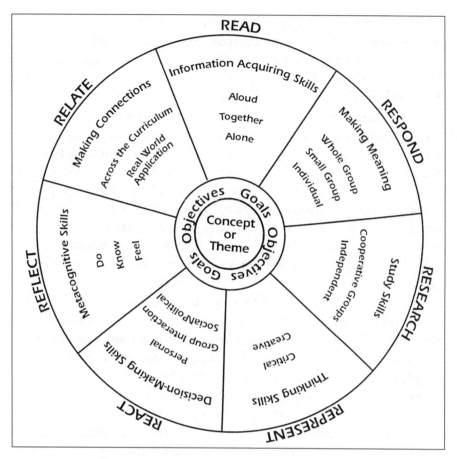

FIGURE 2–2 *The Curriculum Disk*

they've finished planning to check their units. Either way, this template works. Students who have the opportunity to learn through these seven components as they study a social studies theme/concept become more motivated, thoughtful learners.

The Curriculum Disk

The curriculum disk is a planning wheel. Its purpose is to help teachers design integrated curriculum units that put social studies at the center of the school day. The seven components listed are the actions that students should experience when studying a topic in depth. These components represent current best practice in education.

Teachers can begin anywhere on the disk. Some may choose to begin with RELATE, looking immediately for the cross-curricular connections. Others may start with READ, RESEARCH, or REPRE-SENT. It is not necessary to follow the wheel in any particular order but it is important to remember that each of the components con-tributes to another. No one component stands isolated. It is in the blending and mixing of these components that powerful learning and teaching take place. Once an activity is planned within a component doesn't mean that a second activity also highlighting that same com-ponent can't occur later. Often times components are revisited by learners to practice or synthesize a specific skill. It is important to en-sure that students have the opportunity to experience many of the components as they become immersed in a topic.

Certainly the amount of time spent doing each component will vary. Some units lend themselves to a significant amount of time in RESEARCH while others may call upon a major amount of time to be spent in the REACT mode. For example, an introduction to Inuit people may call for a heavy concentration on RESEARCH and REP-RESENT. A unit on hunger may be centered on service learning and what the kids can do about it (REACT). In fact, teachers are encour-aged to vary the time spent, as well as the strategies used, so that so-cial studies learning does not become so predictable that it loses its ability to tantalize the learner. Notice that each of the components is an action verb. This choice is deliberate. It is my experience that stu-dents who are active learners are happier, more motivated, and more productive learners.

READ: *Information Acquiring Skills*

This component includes the development, continued application, and refinement of reading skills, including comprehension, vocabu-lary, and reading rate. Examples of comprehension include differenti-ating between main and subordinate ideas, selecting passages pertinent to the topic studied, and detecting cause-and-effect rela-tionships. Vocabulary skills include the usual word attack skills (sight

FIGURE 2–3   *Annie and Alyssa Discover It Takes Two to Read a Book*

recognition, phonetic analysis, and structural analysis), successful use of context clues, and building a functional word bank of social studies terms. Reading rate requires students to adjust their speed of reading to suit the purpose and difficulty of the material.

For the best results, try identifying three ways students can acquire information about the topic being studied: read alouds, read alones, and read togethers. I like to begin with read alouds, often a picture book about the concept or a novel that connects to the theme in some way. Sometimes the read aloud is a magazine article or a column from a newspaper. Then I like to move to read togethers. This is where I often dip into the textbook, the atlas set we got last year, or those books I have multiple copies of so we can set up book clubs. Finally, I always plan for read alones. These are books that the students choose to read independently on the topic. Frequently I have collections or a list of titles, but much of the time the kids go to the library to find their own books.

RESPOND: *Making Meaning*

"Reading is a meaning-making process: an active, constructive, creative, higher-order thinking activity that involves distinctive cognitive strategies before, during, and after reading" (Zemelman et al. 1998, 30). This component encourages teachers to plan for their students to make meaning at three different organizational levels as they read social studies content: whole group, small group, and individual. Group activities often include brainstorming, listing, categorizing, and discussion. I might ask my kids to list all the events they can recall in Lincoln's life after reading *Lincoln: A Photobiography* (Freedman 1987) aloud to them. After we have listed all the events on the board, I might break them up into small groups and ask them to classify the events into four or five major categories. The third, or individual activity, could be journaling words, phrases, or paragraphs that intrigue, engage, or puzzle the reader. There is no particular order to these organizational constructs. Sometimes I have children read independently first, sometimes last. Since research shows that children tend to use learning strategies in the manner in which the strategies have been taught, think how important it is that we teach reading during social studies using social studies content (Zemelman, et al. 32). If kids only practice reading strategies during reading period, they may not learn how to apply their skills to real-world activities.

RESEARCH: *Study Skills*

Study skills include being able to find information and arrange it in usable forms, as well as being able to use reference and information search skills such as library services, community resources, and technology (Internet and other electronic-information resources). Arranging information in usable forms includes outlines, summaries, time lines, notes, records, reports, research papers, and bibliographies. These skills are most effectively approached through cooperative group work and through independent practice. Often times in my classroom, cooperative group work is used to assist the kids as they develop foundational or basic knowledge about an event or concept. Later in the unit, the kids do independent study in an area that captures their interest. Helping students arrange information in usable forms while focusing on social studies content is one of the most fun things I do as a teacher. There are so many ways to manage information that are creative and stimulating (see Chapter 5 for suggestions). I've found that by keeping assignments relatively contained, perhaps five or six paragraphs, student interest remains high and we have opportunities to practice the skill more than once.

REPRESENT: *Critical and Creative Thinking Skills*

This component is a meaty one. Students organize and use the information they have found and put it into usable forms. Now they may *classify* that information (group data into categories, place information into a sequence, or create a chart). They might *interpret* the information by noting cause-and-effect relationships, draw inferences, or predict likely outcomes. The students could *analyze* information examining the relationships between the elements of the topic being studied or they could compare and contrast credibility of differing accounts of the same event. *Summarizing* information is also an activity that provides higher-level thinking skill application. Here we find students making statements about their conclusions, forming opinions, and stating hypotheses for further study. *Synthesizing* information requires students to make the information their own, to reinterpret or present visually their "take" and to communicate orally or in writing. Students also need practice in *evaluating* information, to determine if it is pertinent to the topic, adequate, and valid. I call these critical thinking skills.

When analyzing the student behaviors that are present in REPRESENT, I find Bellanca and Fogarty's lists of "three-story intellect" verbs particularly helpful in planning:

- Gather, a relatively basic thinking behavior, includes: counting, describing, matching, naming, reciting, selecting, recalling, and telling.
- Process, relatively higher-level thinking activities, includes: comparing, sorting, reasoning, contrasting, solving, distinguishing, classifying, analyzing, and inferring.

- Apply, the highest level of thinking behaviors, includes: evaluating, imagining, judging, predicting, speculating, estimating, forecasting, and supposing. (Bellanca and Fogarty 1991, 300)

Students can represent their grasp of knowledge in a social studies content area through a wide array of projects, papers, and presentations. Creative thinking skills should include opportunities for students to develop their multiple intelligences. Teachers can incorporate visual-spatial activities, music, and movement as well as quiet times for introspection and sharing in a small group. In my classroom, these projects are seldom graded because my students are most often practicing skill development through their representations. They are organizing and using new information, often for the first time. Rather, I assess their ability to stay on task, to work with others, to manage the task and their materials in a time efficient way. I acknowledge their creative gifts and their completion of the task.

Considering the multiple intelligences as I plan my units helps me add variety in my activities and reminds me to include opportunities for all my students to practice different ways of learning and knowing. I often view the multiple intelligences as pigment on an artist's palette from which I can create engaging and informative lessons. In my minds' eye, I view each intelligence (visual-spatial, logical-mathematical, musical, interpersonal, intrapersonal, naturalistic, kinethestic, and linguistic) as a single vivid color. As I construct a unit, I find I seldom use a single color, a lone intelligence, in a lesson. Usually, I blend two or more together to create a worthwhile experience. For example, after my kids have finished reading *The Winter of the Red Snow* (Gregory 1996), a Revolutionary War fictional diary set at Valley Forge, I ask my students to pick a character in the book and write a friendly letter to that character (linguistic). They tell this character what they learned about revolutionary era life from reading this book (intrapersonal). They prioritize three things they think would amaze him or her about today's society (logical-mathematical) and give reasons why. Finally, they write their final draft on stationery they have created that reveals something about them (visual-spatial), construct an envelop to put it in (kinesthetic), and "mail" it to me by a certain due date.

Gardner, in *Frames of Mind* (1985), tells us that:

- The intelligences work together in many ways.
- All people have the ability to develop the intelligences to an adequate level of competency.
- All people have all eight intelligences.
- The intelligences usually work together in complex ways.
- There are many ways to be intelligent within each category— musical, kinesthetic, visual-spatial, interpersonal, intrapersonal, logical-mathematical, linguistic, and naturalist.

Not only do my kids have an opportunity to practice applying various forms of intelligence, but they also produce a product that I can use to assess their grasp of revolutionary times, their comprehension of what they read, their ability to follow directions, the effectiveness of their writing, and their critical thinking skills as they compare a patriot's life to their own lives in contemporary times.

REACT: *Decision-Making Skills*

One way that social studies is different from other disciplines taught during the school day is that there is often a result or response at the conclusion of a unit of study. The kids may identify a situation in which a decision is required. They use their citizenship skills and responsibilities to look at alternative courses of action, make a decision, and then take action to implement that decision. It is important for our students to have practice in making reasoned and informed decisions. To do this they need to develop personal skills such as expressing their own convictions and adjusting their own behavior to fit the dynamics of the group. They need to develop group interaction skills such as contributing to the development of a supportive group climate and serving as a leader or a follower. They also need to practice social and political participation skills such as working to influence those in positions of social power to strive for extensions of freedom, social justice, and human rights. Writing a letter to a newspaper editor, organizing a recycling campaign, collecting food for the hungry, or working to change a law combines skills and disciplines across the curriculum giving our students needed practice in their roles as citizens. It also makes social studies come alive, as part of the real world.

REFLECT: *Thinking About Learning*

Requiring students to become self-observers of their own learning is both powerful and helpful. Whether doing a face-to-face interview, filling out a questionnaire, or writing a reflective journal response, students are empowered when asked to think about their own thinking. We've developed a reflective mantra in our classroom: "What did you do? What did you learn? How do you feel?" Using these three questions, the kids are reminded about the hands-on, doing part of our learning; the heads-on, thinking part; and the hearts-on, feeling part. I'm thinking about adding a fourth question, "What was the

FIGURE 2–4 *Knee-to-Knee, the Kids Respond to Each Other's Research*

most fun?" Brain research is telling us that students learn best in an atmosphere where students feel safe, where they have fun. I've noticed that some kids don't even recognize when they are having fun. They need to think about it later. Bringing back those moments in retrospect builds a positive climate for later learning.

RELATE: *Making Connections*

In the RELATE component of the curriculum disk, teachers are urged to seek out and plan for deliberate connections across the curriculum. This, of all the components, has the potential to interconnect with each of the others. Social studies has a set of essential skills (see the appendix), a body of knowledge, and a mission of promoting civic competence. There are national standards (see Chapter 5) that reflect what social studies educators think is needed to educate citizens to meet the challenge of the future. However, many of the skills are related to skills also required in other disciplines. In today's jam-packed school day, teachers and students need to make efficient use of the little time available. Compressing or connecting curriculum needs is one way to do this. I think of compressing as when the kids are assigned work that provides practice in fundamental skills while using social studies content, for example, practice research skills while delving into a social studies topic that is personally engaging and relates to the theme that is being studied. This way the practice is meaningful in multiple ways and we're compressing the time needed to accomplish two or more tasks.

In my mind, connecting has more to do with tangents. Connecting occurs, for example, when the kids read historical fiction of a period that matches the one we are studying in social studies. The book provides the students with a broader view of an issue, an event or time. Similarly, films, art projects, dramatizations, and music connect the social studies curriculum to kids' lives, or vice versa. More importantly, however, is the realization that practicing a reading skill during social studies is a real-life application of that skill. When kids see the usefulness of the skill, when they experience success using it, they are more likely to try it again in another situation. By consciously seeking connections and giving kids more practice using skills, developing knowledge, and shaping attitudes, we can pack the school day with meaningful, functional, kid-friendly learning.

WOW

Windows on the World (WOW) is the theme of an introductory unit in world geography and world cultures for a four–five combination class. It was planned using the curriculum disk and demonstrates many of the attributes that put social studies at the center of learning in a classroom. It is also the precursor to a second unit, Global Village: Global Vision, which builds and extends upon the student research initiated in Windows on the World. Student application of knowledge is raised to a higher level, requiring critical and creative thinking. The two units demonstrate my belief that students need to see that what they learn in one unit has implications and applications to a different or later unit.

Using the curriculum disk as our guide, let's walk through the planning cycle I followed to provide my students with the world geography and world cultures overview I wanted them to have. Remember, there is no one way to do this planning, no first place you have to start, no sequence you have to follow. This just happens to be what I did for this unit.

When my class did the Windows on the World unit, I had no plans to chronicle it in a book so I didn't keep the rich bits of kids work and comments that always come out of such an activity. I am lucky that one half of my class this year is comprised of kids who participated in that unit over a year ago. Last week, seventeen months later, while most of the class was on a Safety Patrol end-of-the-year outing, I asked the kids if they'd write down what they did, what they learned, and how they felt about the Windows on the World and Global Village units. Their reflections, unedited except for spelling errors, enrich this chapter.

Annie's Reflection

When you open up a window, what do you see? In Mrs. Lindquist's class last year, I looked through many different windows. In them, I could see far off countries and cultures unknown, and the best part was, I made them myself! So after I made the windows, I no longer needed to look in them to see those fascinating places. I could forever carry them with me in my mind, and unlike most things, I would never forget them.

I used to think geography was very dull. Just open up a textbook and read about some boring old economy! But creating my windows on the world was like writing my *own* textbook. And it could be however I wanted it to be. With colorful postcards and games like true or false. And when I finished, my mind was just bursting with fun facts. I mean, who would have thought that in Finland, there are imaginary critters called Moomans that supposedly protect the forest? And knowledge wasn't the only thing buzzing through my mind. Pride was filling me up to the brim, and when I looked at those pages of windows, I felt like a million dollars. Who knows, maybe I'll go to those places some day . . .

WOW: *Read*

If someone were to ask me how my teaching has changed in the last ten years, I would be able to respond immediately. First, Howard Gardner's theory of multiple intelligences has profoundly affected the way I teach and my kids learn. Second, picture books flood my classroom and every concept or theme we explore begins with a story. So we begin Windows on the World with stories from different countries around the world. These stories have the power to teach my kids, revealing values of far-away countries, unveiling distant landscapes, and introducing new ways of looking at things. Our best bet is hitting the picture book section of the school library. By using picture story books, students can find legends, folktales, or fairy tales from countries that are at their reading comfort level. After reading a story, students prepare storyboards, analyzing the story using the six elements of fiction. (See storyboard directions in *Seeing the Whole Through Social Studies*.) After reading and enjoying each other's storyboards, we categorize the stories by continent and look for similarities and differences. One of the most revealing questions we examine is, "What do you think you would learn if you were a child of this particular country and you heard this particular story many times?" We discuss how stories often teach the listener proper ways to behave or warn us of dangers in the land. My students frequently share personal stories their families tell. These personal stories can become writing exercises practicing voice or word choice, trying out "hooks" for openings or developing interesting conclusions.

WOW: *Respond*

There's no way that every one of my kids can study every single country in the world, know the geography of each, and have some appreciation for the individual cultures. So what do I want them to know? What do they want to know?

- location, including neighboring countries
- well-known landmarks such as Mt. Everest or the Mediterrean Sea
- general geographic regions and place markers such as peninsulas and plains
- plants, animals, and natural resources that are abundant or unique
- cultural characteristics that intrigue, engage, and inform

We don't spend time memorizing locations, such a capital cities. Instead I teach my students how to use a "global address," those lattitudinal and longitudinal grid lines that specifically identify any place on earth. We play games, learning to find places, beginning to generalize about what kind of geographic conditions we may find at a given latitude and longitude. Hours, minutes, and seconds take on new meanings. The twenty-four hour clock, Greenwich mean time, and crossing the international dateline become useful concepts. My belief is that, while it's wonderful for a kid to know where some place is, it's even better when he or she knows how to find it. Atlases, wall maps, and computers all contribute to my students' developing abilities to find any place on earth.

Living in the Northwest, we decide to start with the continent closest to us, Asia. Getting out the atlases again, and pulling down the world map, we make some generalizations about Asia based on what we observe on a physical map and comparing it geographically

FIGURE 2–5 *Betsy Researches the Country of Her Choice*

with the Northwest. We review how to interpret the legend and use the compass rose. Countries are named and located. Then each student chooses a country to investigate. (It's all right if more than one child chooses the same country.) Brainstorming things we might like to know, we develop a country profile to guide individual research.

WOW: Research

My students and I discuss what we think might be important or interesting to know and decide on the following, with the understanding that no one needs to find them all:

capital

official language(s)

population

land area

elevation—highest and lowest

climate and seasons

notable landmarks, including significant lakes and rivers

chief products, including agriculture, manufacturing, forestry, fishing, and mining

housing—city and rural

typical foods

work

recreation

religion

education

the arts

rare or endangered animals and plants

transportation

history

problems that people face

Research skills are critical to the students' success. Knowing where to look, how to look, identifying key words, organizing information, and determining what guiding questions to ask are skills that need to be modeled or reviewed.

My students choose among several avenues of research. Some use Encarta and/or Grolier's on the computer. Others head for the library to look for nonfiction reference books about the country. My challenge is to encourage quick, current, comprehensive data acquisition without plagiarism. My way of helping students avoid copying directly from the screen or the page is to ask them to create a list of "fast facts"—none of which may be a complete sentence, none of which may be word processed. I've found that writing by hand helps my kids practice note taking during this first project. The students will create at least four Windows on the World, and the requirements will change as we progress.

In terms of integration, my kids practice the reading skill of identifying the most important part of a statement and summarizing while note taking. I also encourage my students to check out print resources such as encyclopedias and *National Geographic*. For students whose reading skills are not comprehensive or who may lack the confidence or skill to deal with diverse information, individual country books with lots of pictures and boldly identified important information contribute significantly to their success.

Three Tiers of Research

The fast-facts strategy requires students to use relatively basic thinking skills at what I call the first tier of research. It requires them to find and import data from a reference source to their own paper as they become familiar with the geographic, economic, and cultural "outline" of the country they have chosen to explore. This is an ideal time to plan a museum field trip or to invite in a cultural speaker if possible. Playing music from other countries as the kids come in each morning stimulates some students. Photographs encourage others to dig for data.

The objective of the second tier of research involves learning more about the culture, to begin to appreciate intellectually and emotionally the inhabitants and their ways of life. The Internet has been a good resource for my students, especially with the child-safe search engines like Yahooligans.com, kidinfo.com, and bonus.com. *Material World* (available on CD-ROM as well as bound) and *Children Like Me*, plus magazines like *National Geographic* help my kids begin to identify with those who live in the country they are investigating. Building a visual repertoire is important to creating a connection between the children and the cultures they are studying. Questions, posed by both the kids and me, guide research during this time.

What do the people like?

What makes life easy or hard for them?

How is their life like or not like ours?

What would you enjoy most about visiting this country?

Ideally, the kids will be able to answer these kinds of questions at the completion of their study. I also ask the kids to note any particular problems people are struggling with in that country, whether it be war, famine, depletion of natural resources, or natural disasters. I encourage the kids, and their families, to check local newspapers for articles about their country. Making a scrapbook page of these articles is often very revealing and informational. The questions provide an informal assessment for me to use as I walk around the room, engaging the kids in conversation about their research. In addition, I structure small-group conversations so the kids can share their insights with each other, comparing and contrasting conditions in the different countries.

The third and final tier of research is more cumulative, more generalized, higher-level thinking. I ask the kids to think about what they would show a visitor from that country if they came to visit our community and why. This is one kind of assessment I use to check student comprehension of how the subject matter connects to their own lives.

Other Resources

Some of my students seldom get past the first tier of research during this first Window on the World. That's okay with me. Their reading and writing skills are such that they are working hard to simply find those facts. However, often by the last Window on the World, these kids are able to join in more complex tasks. The repetitive nature of this unit provides students plenty of practice. Their research skills sharpen, their reading often improves, they see many models of alternative ways to organize material, and they hear many examples of higher-level thinking. Plus, there are some students who start from generalizations and then move to the fact level. Connections for these kinds of learners is more likely to happen, I've found, if I have lots of picture resources. If all they have is print, whether electronic or paper, then their reading level traps them. However, if they can access pictures and photographs, they are often more successful. Some possible technology resources follow:

- *Neighborhood Map Machine*, an easy-to-use tool (by Tom Snyder Productions) that enables students and teachers to create, navigate, and print maps of their own neighborhoods or imaginary places using objects such as roads, trees, lakes, buildings, and parks. It prints maps in regular or poster size. The price is $79.95. Recommended for grades 1–5. Available from http://cdl-cambridge.com, or 800-637-0047.
- *GeoSafari Geography* is a CD-ROM program in which your students will travel the world and be challenged on everything from currencies, flags, and world landmarks to U.S. states and capitals. The price is $29.95. Recommended for grades 3–12. Available from http://cdl-cambridge.com, or 800-637-0047.
- *Picture Atlas of the World* is a multimedia atlas with maps of every nation containing color photographs of each country's people, places, and landforms. Students have access to more than eight hundred interactive maps, twelve hundred full-color photographs, audio and video clips, and information on the newest countries. The price is $79.95. Recommended for grades 4–12. Available from http://cdl-cambridge.com, or 800-637-0047.

WOW: *Represent*

Representing-to-learn demonstrates the students' comprehension of the theme or concept. Understandings and misunderstandings are revealed through student drawings, writings, and construction. Several years ago, writing-to-learn (Elbow 1973 and Fulwiler 1987) was identified as a powerful way to assess student comprehension. From writing-to-learn, other forms of communication are now validated as evidence of what kids know. Representing-to-learn was coined by

Zemelman et al. in *Best Practices: New Standards for Teaching and Learning in America's Schools*, 2nd Edition.

Based on our initial list of what we thought was important, it seems reasonable to start by having students reproduce a map of their chosen country. For many of my fourth graders, an outline of the country that is reasonably accurate and one that identifies major cities, bodies of water, geographic regions and includes a legend and a compass rose is fine with me. More advanced students can reproduce physical maps in greater detail. We start with what I call "eye drawing"—looking at a map and drawing it as best as they can. By the last map, the kids are using grid lines to scale their drawings, much like latitude and longitude lines.

Using 12" × 18" white construction paper, I give my students time to draw a physical map of their chosen country, showing them

FIGURE 2–6 *Getting Reactions from Their Second-Grade Buddies, Jordan and Mackenzie*

models of how to label clearly. I have found that if I provide fine-tip black felt pens, their labels will be legible. I encourage students to use a straight edge when labeling. After looking at various compass roses on a variety of maps, requiring a compass rose and encouraging creativity is fun for most kids as well as educational. Similarly, legends are incorporated. I also require the country name to be clearly visible. I emphasize that this map needs to be sizable (large enough so that we can learn from it easily), neat (we can read it clearly), fairly accurate (we can get a pretty good idea of where things are), and colorful and attractive (we are attracted by this presentation). If at all possible, the kids try to position their maps in the middle of the 18" wide paper. If there is time, students may add any details, such as borders or a flag, that they wish.

I like to think of the map as the beginning. It is, in fact, a real window on the world. But what can we learn looking through that window?

Organizational Skills: Going Through the Window

When a student finishes a map, we cut it in to two 9-inch halves. My students staple these two halves on to a second piece of 12" × 18" construction paper on the outer, 12-inch edge. Carefully folding the map paper back, they create a "window." Now the kids learn more about the geography and how the environment shapes the cultures of that country. This is where the kids have an opportunity to explore and examine information that has captured their interest. For example, using the Internet, many of the kids find recipes for traditional food, some in the language of the country they are researching. Several of the kids draw flags, stamps, and/or currency facsimiles. Some cut pictures out of old *National Geographic* magazines I have saved. A few kids create a traveler's journal, as if they are on holiday. Others make a stack of postcards representing sites they would like to visit. A couple of kids rewrite legends they've found. One girl shares an interview with her grandmother, an immigrant from her selected county. In fact, throughout the Windows on the World project, many of the students choose to study a country that has personal meaning for them, whether their families had emigrated from the country, or traveled to the country, or, as one child put it, "I like the food."

The purpose of the segments put inside the window is to inform, enrich, and engage us, as a class. The segments I've listed above are just a few of the creative pieces my students devised. Each time someone thinks of a new segment, someone else piggybacks on that idea and carries it a bit further. It is fun, creative, educational . . . and fits our curriculum. My students can't wait for WOW time every day and neither can I! Like Alice in Wonderland, we have an adventure every time we go "through our windows."

WOW: *React*

Our next step is to find a primary class with which to share our windows. I am a firm believer in the research that shows we learn what we teach. Having intermediate students take their window to another classroom and share their knowledge is very powerful—for both sets of students. The older student is validated for creating a useful and attractive product and has an opportunity to share knowledge in addition to the product. The younger student gets a glimmer of what's ahead and begins to recognize that studies, like geography, are important; skills, like organization and management of materials, do affect the outcome; and sharing knowledge is a powerful and fun way to learn.

When my class gets back from sharing with a younger group, I always give them time to debrief, to share their observations and to make comments. Then they share with each other. Sitting knee-to-knee in groups, my kids share their windows, learning from each other. Not only do they learn about other countries on the same continent, but they see alternative organizational strategies, observe art techniques, and store these ideas away for the next window they will create. This is one way to improve overall product quality. Models for kids, especially those who find this kind of activity challenging, provides structure and a plan for the second window assignment. Lastly, every single window is displayed on the bulletin board and around the room and students are encouraged to browse through them.

Mackenzie's Reflection

Oh man! I learned zillions of things!

When Mrs. Lindquist's 4–5 combination class started our Windows on the World projects, I knew very little about other countries. My first window was sloppy, had little information, and had white spaces galore.

As time went on, my pages got fuller, as did my brain. I put flip pages on the inside of my windows as well as physical and political maps on the outside. My fast facts are colorfully decorated, and, oh, a border around that picture. Hmmm, maybe I'll put a border around all the pictures. This one red, that one green. Yes! Finally finished. I feel like a leaf that had been laying on the ground, now swept up into the air.

The projects were both fun and hard. After the last one was completed, I felt tired and happy. I was happy that I had done it all but sad there were no more windows.

WOW: *Reflect*

Time to move to a second continent, choose a new country, and create a second window. One of the major values of this unit is that students get to do almost the same assignment four times as we work our way around the continents: 1) Asia; 2) Europe; 3) Canada, Mexico, and the Caribbean; and 4) South America. This repetition gives students time to modify and explore techniques, offers the opportunity to expand and make more efficient their research, provides models so their maps are increasingly more accurate, and encourages increased creativity in the pieces added through the windows. Each time, however, the assignment criterion is altered, gradually increasing the level of difficulty, asking for evidence of using an increased number of the multiple intelligences. For instance, I might ask for a descriptive paragraph, or require at least one three-dimensional piece.

First window criteria

- Eye-draw a pictorial or physical map. Outline in black pen. Color.
- Create four informational sections, using four topics from the country profile.

Second window criteria
- Eye draw a pictorial or physical map. Outline in black. Color.
- Create four informational sections, two of which are different from your first. One of your sections must utilize an application of technology (Internet download, etc.).

Third window criteria
- Create a physical or political map using grid lines. Outline in black. Color.
- Create four informational sections, two of which are different from your first and second window. One of your sections must use a pop-up or pop-out strategy.

Fourth window criteria
- Create a product or political map, using grid lines. Outline in black. Color.
- Write a research paper about any country in South America. Add a geography reference. You may want to add an introduction and a conclusion. Refer to *Writer's Express* (Kemper et al. 1995) for opening "hooks," satisfying conclusions, and transition words.
- Create two informational sections in addition to your research paper.

Each country study reflects a slightly revised window. My students have an opportunity to choose among pictorial maps, political, physical, or product maps. By the time we get to South America, the kids are skilled researchers. Up to this point, their research has been very graphic, very pictorial, often kinesthetic. Now seems like a good time to turn their research from graphic displays to written reports.

We skip Antarctica and Australia since our K–5 curriculum encompasses those continents. I also decide to save Africa for the spring so we can combine the geography of Africa with science studies of endangered species and rain forests. We do not spend time on the United States since it is covered later.

FIGURE 2–7 *Calista Compares and Contrasts Peer's WOW. Projects as She Reflects on Her Own Accomplishments*

WOW: *Relate*

So, what connections have we made in this unit? There are a host of required language-arts skills that have been introduced or reviewed, applied, practiced, and elaborated:

choosing appropriate sources for research

reading books, newspapers, and periodicals

adjusting reading rate for purpose

retelling a story

analyzing a story by using the six elements of fiction

taking notes

organizing information

presenting information in an engaging and informative way

writing paragraphs

writing introductions that engage the reader

summarizing information

using proper conventions

listening

Specific art skills include lettering, devising and using borders, and using a grid to increase or decrease the size of an image. Mathematical-logical skills include organizing information sequentially, distinguishing between different kinds of maps, comparing and contrasting information from country to country, and laying out a graphic presentation in a sequential manner. One basic intermediate-middle-school requirement that combines almost all of these skills is the research paper.

Data Sheets

Over the years, I've observed that students do better reseach writing when they have a body of knowledge to write about. Because of that, I have developed what I call data sheets to guide beginning research writers. The first data sheet handed to my students is a General Data Sheet and includes space for information more geographic in nature. The students determine what they think is interesting and what they want to know about the geography of their chosen country. The general data sheet acts as a guide, not a police officer, as the kids build a knowledge base about their country of choice:

capital	official language(s)
population	land area
elevation	landmarks
climate and weather	endangered animals and plants
oceans, lakes, rivers	geographic regions

I do not give the children a whole lot of room to write their findings, so they often write only words and phrases. No complete sentences are required on a data sheet. Just the facts.

Once again, my students use a variety of resources including the Internet, electronic encyclopedias, and print resources. A few minutes to review how to use each of the resources available is time well spent. Asking students to demonstrate the use of various resources in a "goldfish bowl" has proven effective in my classroom. (The goldfish bowl technique is when a student or group of students performs the task or activity with all the other students sitting around them, watching. This technique is especially effective when the student[s] or teacher debrief at the end of the demonstration, pointing out critical components of the task.)

When the first data sheet is completed, we move to cultural data. Now the students pose questions and find information about what interests them culturally. Many of the questions focus on the following topics:

housing	food	recreation	religious/beliefs
education	the arts	heroes or	highlights of the
		celebrities	history

The third data sheet focuses on economics. Students can research any of the topics below or ones that they choose themselves:

mining	forestry	fishing	manufacturing
agriculture	imports	exports	natural resources
technology	work (cities, rural)		transportation

Because the children have been doing essentially this same research in graphic detail for earlier windows, each data sheet is completed fairly quickly and quite accurately.

Putting away all reference materials except for the data sheets, my students begin writing up their research instead of displaying it graphically. Each data sheet provides ample information to write a meaty paragraph. Using *Writer's Express* (Kemper et al. 1995), a superlative student writing guide book, the children attend to writing skills such as adding transition words. The class discusses whether metaphors or similes would be effective. The kids practice what they need to: varying sentence structure, expanding some sentences, or beginning sentences in different ways. I provide minilessons on each of the skills.

Some students finish three paragraphs and are satisfied. Some add additional paragraphs. We discuss whether an introduction or conclusion is needed. Conclusions and introductions often tap into the second and third tiers of research, in which students demonstrate

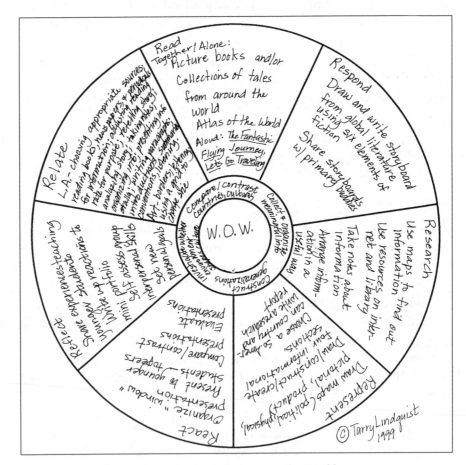

FIGURE 2–8 *Curriculum Disk for Windows on the World*

their ability to analyze and summarize. Finding just the right introductory "hook" for the reader is a real intellectual adventure for some young writers. Donald Graves (1994) suggests that about 80 percent of all writing should be student choice and 20 percent teacher choice. This assignment blends teacher strategy and student choice.

This year, we went from handwritten research data sheets to composing directly on the word processor. It was surprisingly successful, and revising was a realistic, worthwhile activity. But in all past years my students have handwritten their reports. While it's nice for the students to have a choice, technology facilitates revision. Word processing makes it easier to rewrite or reorganize one's writing. The writing process is less onerous and more efficient thanks to the computer, especially for those students for whom handwriting is difficult. Many of us have technology standards to meet. The research report provides another possible and welcome integration.

In this social studies-centered unit, a major connection is that between social studies and the communication skills of research writing. Nonfiction writing is a critical skill to success in social studies through the grades.

Assessment: Putting It All Together

In addition to their research report, my students draw one last map and create a window for their South American country. They staple their research report inside the window and add two sections of information. After sharing with peers, two pieces of tagboard become the cover and back of their Windows on the World project book. Stapled only on the left side, these covers protect all four country projects. Ordered from first (Asia) to last one completed (South America), the windows project book also provides a mini-portfolio of student progress. Certainly, their final window demonstrates increased expertise in ability to research, organize, and present material.

The kids help with the assessment. While each country Window on the World had its own separate rubric and the students received grades for each one, putting them all together creates a new product. However, more than a grade, I am interested in the kids reflecting on the work and their work habits, to identify what they learned, to review what they did, and to express how they feel about this body of work. (See Window on the World checklist in the Appendix.)

Reading and Writing

Creating the four windows, and consequently studying four continents, takes us almost three months. As a self-contained classroom teacher, I am expected to teach other subjects besides social studies. But many of those other things I'm supposed to teach appear in our social studies windows project. In addition to the note taking, summarizing, and research skills the kids practiced, they were also continuing to read about countries around the world, working on nonfiction reading skills. I encourage the kids to find books about people who live in other cultures or who explore other places in the world. I challenge them to read about heroes and leaders from around the world. I bring in nonfiction books, many that deal with geography and history.

Folktales, legends, and myths were often the books of choice during reader's workshop. Whether in picture-book format or a collection, these shorter stories were engaging to many of my kids. To monitor the reading, I provided a menu of written and graphic reading responses the kids could choose from as they wrote daily in their reading journals that ranged from retelling to summarizing, analyzing, and evaluating. I worked hard at conferencing with each child once a week.

At the beginning of the year, my goal is basic: to get my students to put their responses on paper. I am quite flexible about format, handwriting style, and length. As the weeks tick by, I gradually cinch up the requirements as I observe the levels of confidence and competency increase.

In addition to reading and writing about countries around the world, I decide to throw in a spelling connection. Although my regular spelling program doesn't include the countries of the world, it seems to me that my students can give the world list a whirl. We take with distinct cultures. They had to apply what they knew about musical structure and notation to write lyrics and compose scores. They also had to utilize performance skills.

Art and drama skills were tapped. Whether creating a poster urging support for a global issue or creating a play to demonstrate the consequences of inaction, the kids drew on previous practice, new insights, and increasing skills in the arts.

And of course, the language-arts skills are the bedrock of this unit, as with most social studies units: process and performance skills, script writing, research, expressing personal convictions, business letters, persuasive paragraphs. . . . Put it all together and what have we got: a highly integrated, kid-focused, social studies centered, worthwhile unit that provides students with a lifelong model for investigating issues and determining personal opinions using intellectual tools rather than knee-jerk emotions.

Betsy's Reflection

Looking back on what we did, two things pop into my mind: Windows on the World and Global Village. For Windows on the World, each person in class chose a country from Europe, Asia, North America, and South America, and did a window on it. In doing this, I learned facts about each country that I did (Azerbaijan, Sweden, El Salvador, and Peru) and I learned some organization skills, which I enriched throughout the year and into this next year. I feel good about what I accomplished, and everything I learned and have still to learn. Making those Windows on the World was amazing, and it enriched our minds and imaginations. When you looked through someone's window, you could imagine the culture and the people that you see and read about.

The Global Village was much different, working in groups of four or five, each group chose a global problem and did a presentation on it and how you could help get rid of it by using posters, making plays, and talking about it to the class. My group focused on refugees and we did play about a girl's family having to leave because of war. It was very interesting and educational but the best part was that it was probably one of the funnest projects of the year.

it one continent at a time and spend two to three weeks on each list. I like my students to be able to identify the name of a country and place it in context.

Art

In art, the kids are applying graphic design skills as they create their windows. These skills range from using borders to define areas often incorporating appropriate ethnic touches, placing information in an eye-appealing way, and experimenting with lettering styles to cutting pictures out neatly, gluing the whole picture onto the window instead of hitting a little glue in the center, and writing labels level instead of uphill. They are encouraged to experiment with three-dimensional pieces, such as scrolls tied onto a window segment, multipaged booklets, and pockets with interesting information resting inside.

Final Assessment

The final assessment is reflective in nature. Students sit at their desks, Window on the World portfolio in front of them. Each receives a piece of paper with the following directions:

Using your portfolio,

1. List five ways that the countries you studied are similar. Explain why or give evidence.
2. List five ways they are different. Explain why or give evidence.
3. If a guest came from each of the countries you studied to visit Washington state, what do you think each of them would be most interested in seeing? (List no more than four items total. Give reasons for your choices.)

Moving On, Moving Up

Many teachers would stop at the end of this unit and feel they had served their students well in terms of familiarizing them with world geography. That was my own original intent. Yet, when we finished our Windows on the World, it seemed to me that we had just paved the way for some exciting, higher-level thinking. Windows on the World is a perfect platform from which to explore global issues. In 1981, I wrote my first deliberately integrated social studies unit. I called it Global Visions. After writing that unit I got involved with our state social studies council and eventually, the National Council for the Social Studies. Over the years I continued to do Global Visons with my students, always stopping after the creation of the global village. I guess I realized that we really couldn't go on because my kids didn't have enough background to tackle more. Windows on the World, however, provided the very scaffold my young students needed to take the next step, to examine global issues. Because of the group of kids I had and due to my own interest as well, we moved seamlessly to a new, revised version of the Global Visions unit. The revised version, "Global Village, Global Vision" follows. Windows on the World could certainly stand alone as a worthwhile unit. In more advanced classes, so could Global Village, Global Vision. However, with my four–five split class, the two together became one unit. Windows on the World provided the familiarity and background needed to move into the higher level skills required by Global Village, Global Visions. A detailed curriculum disk for each of the units illustrates the thoughts and strategies used for guiding the kids through to understanding the concepts.

George's Reflection

Whoa, wow, hard, fun, awesome! It was the day, the day Mrs. Lindquist introduced our first project of the year, Windows on the World. At first I thought, how am I going to draw the map and the flag? It seemed so hard.

Maybe I should rewind.

A Window on the World is a book with a map and a flag of a country on the front, then when you open it up, it has different things like fast facts or true or false. Sometimes it has pictures and made-up postcards from that country. All these things are to help the viewer learn. I think making these books helped me learn about a lot of different countries and I am glad we did this project. Looking back on it now makes me wonder if I can still draw that well and gather up information that easily. Maybe I shouldn't say easily. It was very challenging. It was very fun. And I wish I could do it again.

Global Village, Global Vision

Most elementary curriculum guides ignore global issues. Yet, it is one of the ten key standards included in the National Council for the Social Studies *Expectations for Excellence*. I work on global issues in my classroom because my kids learn important critical-thinking skills, practice organizational and presentation skills, and experience a current, worthwhile connection with the world in which they live. And recently, I learned how global issues can become a conduit for planned, specific everyday conversation between student and parent about school curriculum.

At the 1997 National Council for the Social Studies conference, I heard Dr. Janet Alleman from Michigan State University talk about a technique she and her colleague, Dr. Jere Brophy, had been investigating. She called it Out-of-School Learning and described in some detail how this strategy was being explored to invite families to be more a part of the everyday school curriculum. I liked what she said and thought that it would be a useful strategy, bridging that home–school gap. What I have done is applied my understanding of this strategy to my classroom. Each day an interview question connected to current curriculum goes home. Someone in the family should be able to answer it without special knowledge or resources. It is very important that the students have an opportunity to share the results of their interviews the next day as a part of regular class work.

How to begin this phase of our study? I wanted to capitalize on my students' newfound knowledge and interest in the world. I believe that what we do in class should be useful to the kids, that they should be able to move to deeper levels of knowing, broader reaches of understanding because of what they do in class. The question is: What would be a natural extension of the WOW project? Could we build a global village? Would using the windows unit as a framework help the students gain global vision?

Identifying Climatic Zones (Read)

Using the Internet (www.timelifeedu.com) and print resources to check out climatic zones, the students identify key climatic zones. Since these vary slightly from source to source, my students choose temperate, tropical, polar, arid, Mediterranean, and mountain zones.

The Windows unit stands the kids in good stead as they meet in small groups, listing the attributes they think characterize a specific zone. I can hear the kids contributing from their newly acquired prior knowledge of different countries. Investigating different climatic zones begins. Books like *Ali, Child of the Desert*, by Jonathan London (Lothrop: 1997), in which the impact of the desert on Berber traditions and culture is clearly felt, and *Storm on the Desert*, by Carolyn Lesser (Harcourt Brace: 1997), in which poetic narrative and dynamic watercolors record the passage of a violent desert storm, are two of the picture books we find.

Using butcher paper, the kids list all the facts they can find about a specific climatic zone. That afternoon, I set up the first family interview question, treating it as homework. Providing a copy for every child, I emphasize the importance this information will have to the success of our study. To encourage the students to actually interview their families, points will be awarded for participation each day. (We define family as "anyone you live with.") The questions are structured to not put anyone on the spot, regardless of wealth, education, or other socioeconomic factors. In this case, the family interview question is: How does climate affect our lives?

Creating Critters (Respond)

We start the day by sharing family interviews and listing the effects on butcher paper for future reference. Answers such as, "we have a furnace," "we have to buy coats," "we need to protect ourselves from the weather," are listed. The discussion reinforces the kids who remembered and encourages those who didn't to participate in the future.

Using a physical or climatic map, we identify general climatic zones around the world. The kids point out well-known cities and familiar places in each zone based, once again, on their windows unit. I place students randomly in groups and assign each group a zone. (If your groups are too big, make doubles of some zones. For example, we had two tropical groups to keep our group size at four students.)

Now for the fun. I give each student a walnut and demonstrate how to crack it in half. (It's good to have extras because some will break.) Using tempera paint, markers, bits of felt and yarn, glue, and googily eyes from a craft shop, each student creates at least two critters out of walnut halves. Some may have time to do more. If walnuts aren't readily available, try clay. The students bring empty milk cartons from lunch, rinsing them out with water and drying overnight. Or they may use individual-sized cereal boxes to build houses for their critters. The family interview question is, "How would our lives change if we lived in a different climatic zone?"

FIGURE 2–9 *Bryan's Critters Are Ready to Go*

Rachael's Reflection

The global village was really fun and interesting. What we did was we took walnut shell halves and we turned them into creatures by painting them and then gluing on eyes and pieces of felt. Then we made them houses out of cereal boxes and created countries.

One of the things I learned was that when different countries are close together, problems tend to start quickly, and over small things. I also learned that if you want to have a successful country, it is probably a good idea to cooperate with other countries.

I feel I learned a lot during this period that was really worth learning. Global village was terrific!

Climatically Correct Critter Houses (Respond)

After sharing responses from family, we begin the day with each group reviewing what they have learned about their assigned climatic zone. We rearrange desks so members of each group are sitting together and the kids "introduce" their critters to each other. My kids have names for each critter. Some of them invent histories and most become incredibly attached to their critters. There's a whole raft of language-arts activities that the critters make possible, such as diaries, letters, poems, and narratives for making literacy connections.

What is a basic need of all critters? Shelter. How can we use the empty milk cartons to create an appropriate dwelling for the critters? Using picture books, I spend a few minutes contrasting a house in the polar zone to one in the tropical zone. We explore how the building materials would differ from zone to zone based on the available natural resources. The groups begin to work on climatically correct houses for their critters, made from the milk or cereal cartons. One group of kids decides to tape their cartons together to make an apartment building to save room in their country for wild creatures. I overhear another group planning to bring in an oatmeal box to provide a tower for a runway. Best of all, the kids really reflect their understanding of how climate influences the way people live. The tropical houses are open to the breezes, made of natural fibers and placed near the lagoon. The arctic houses hunker down in their surroundings, blending in, becoming part of the landscape. Tonight's family interview question is, "What would or would not be in our house if we lived in the tropical zone?"

Houses Done, Countries Begun! (Research)

Once again, we begin the day by discussing the family interview question. I like what is happening. This strategy provides a way to foster input into the day by my students' families. The kids like it, too. Their families are becoming a part of our daily conversation, input is valued and used, and a wider range of ideas is put on table to explore. More significantly, my kids are thinking about what we are doing during off-school hours. They are mentally meeting and manipulating ideas that impact our work in school.

Students are encouraged to finish their dwellings today so they can share their creations with the whole class, explaining those nuances we can't immediately see. Although a tropical hut may look low-tech, we are soon informed as to its twenty-first–century modifications, including digital television and cell phones. We spend time identifying how the dwellings are alike and how they are different. I don't know what I value more: the creativity of the kids or the cohesive vision of the groups. Both are worthwhile and wonderful.

Focusing on their climatic zone, the students will be creating a new country tomorrow. They need to be thinking of a name for this country. The family interview question for tonight is, "What is one problem that you think countries in my assigned climatic zone face?"

After school I lay out the countries. Liking the kids to work on tables, I borrow folding tables from the PTA for a couple of weeks. But this activity can take place on the floor. An area about 8' × 12' (four 3' × 8' tables pushed together) covered with butcher paper provides a surface on which to create one huge map of the countries.

I outline each country on the butcher paper, creating at least one island and one landlocked country. For example, I usually make the northern-most country polar, the island tropical, and the

Mediterranean and temperate countries neighbors, sharing a border. I like to make the Mediterranean country with ample coastline and often make the arid country landlocked.

The kids will work around the tables, weaving in and out of each other's way as they customize their countries. Remember, this activity can also be placed on the floor. Just be sure to put it where it can remain for two to three weeks.

Creating a Global Country . . . Groups Make It Easier and More Difficult! (React)

This is a good day to try to have a relatively long, uninterrupted block of time or plan to continue the activity over several days. Planning an hour-and-a-half work time means leaving something else out for the day! That's okay occasionally. In fact, we don't do a formal science curriculum during this unit. Everything is wrapped around this extension of "Windows on the World." When this unit is completed, our days will center in much the same fashion on a required science concept.

After listing problems from the most recent family interview question on chart paper, we go on a "walk about" around the country map. Looking at the two-dimensional representation of their new country, the kids begin to brainstorm ways to make the countries more reflective of their climatic zone. Their assignment is to paint their country, place their houses and critters in their country, and add any details they want. Then I get out the way!

Working in groups provides the support some kids sorely need. My kids work with enthusiasm and energy. Peace reigns for a while, but sooner or later, someone infringes on another country's space and the friction begins. For example, the group with the landlocked country has to lean over and/or work around the countries that surround them. Group work suddenly makes the task more difficult.

With the first outburst, I stop the whole class. Putting down the paint and paper, we sit on the floor and discuss what is happening. Should we ignore it or intervene? Usually the answer will be, "ignore." The kids are so busy they want to get back to work. So we do.

Each group names their country and creates characteristics that support their vision.

Inevitably, problems escalate and it is necessary to have a sit-down discussion again. My kids observe that their problems (border conflicts, encroachment, and so forth) mimic real global issues. The emotional investment the kids have in their countries also mimics national loyalties. We look at causes and effects. We brainstorm solutions because the only other alternative seems to be war. The global village is beginning to provide global vision. Tonight's family interview question is, "What can countries do who are having problems with other countries?"

Determining the Data (React)

As groups put final touches on their countries, the students read and share knowledge they have collected about real countries in their assigned climatic zone. They get out their WOW products, pointing out photographs or checking data they investigated earlier. Their businesslike demeanor as they hunt through their windows and their joy when they find that elusive fact reinforces my belief that a worthwhile unit should be constructed so students will use prior research, their *own* research, for further study. It validates their effort and shows that research is important. Research is not an end in itself. Research forms the foundation for problem solving. When all groups have completed their tasks, we discuss the family interview question and add any more alternatives the students generate.

The next phase of this build-your-own-global-village process begins with the introduction of the country-chart activity. On one side of a large piece of tagboard, the kids create a flag with their country name. On the other side, they come to agreement on specific data about their country: language, education, favorite foods, natural resources, form of government, holidays, exports, and imports. Lots of negotiating goes on during this time, along with lots of laughter. The air is almost electric with the creativity and ideas that are flowing. Most groups come to closure fairly rapidly since they have been shaping their countries and sharing ideas as they work on the global map. Using string through paper-punched holes, the charts are suspended from the metal supports that hold up the acoustical ceiling tile, hanging above each country. Tonight's family interview question is, "Name as many global issues as you can."

Possible global issues

droughts	avalanches	wars	volcanoes
no agriculture	blizzards	housing shortage	windstorms
global warming	tidal waves	population	earthquakes
poverty	territorial issues	monsoons	frozen pipes
starvation	orphans	endangered species	*el niño*
refugees	racism	governments	child labor
education	slavery	individual rights	landfills
water pollution	deforestation	landmines	air pollution
sandstorms	flooding	hurricanes	chemical weapons
virus	transportation	frostbite	acid rain
snowbound	snow removal	threats or instability	
insect-borne diseases			

Making Music (Represent)

After listing all the global issues named as a result of the family interview, the kids and I discuss what is meant by local, regional, and global. We try to categorize the list above using those three classifications. It's an imperfect task, but does demonstrate how point of view shapes decision making very vividly. Issues often end up in two or three categories. It's time to add another piece to the country-chart assignment. I ask the groups to create a national anthem for their country and be ready to share it in the next few days. Many of my fifth graders are taking band for the first time and they are anxious to play their instruments. Others begin creating their lyrics, borrowing the music from published songs. Some decide on a blend; they'll make up words to songs they already know how to play in band. It's amazing how versatile the tune "Hot Cross Buns" can become!

Meanwhile, I copy the list of global issues from the board and make a handout for the kids to take home tonight. The family interview question is, "Out of this list, what do you think are the top three global issues?"

Maryn's Reflection

Doing Windows on the World was actually preparation for what we did next, the Global Village and learning about world problems. We created walnut creatures, homes, and whatever else we thought our country needed. When we were done creating our village, we made posters with our flag, language, government, foods, climate, exports, imports, and our national anthem. The next step was to pick a world problem with your group, teach the class about it and give solutions to the problem. I learned that some of the things I do every day that I've never thought twice about affect the environment and myself.

By doing just the village part, I understand more about how people get into wars. If I am hanging over somebody's country and they don't want me there we'll get into an argument. If we can't come up with a solution . . .

Last year after we did Windows on the World, I felt like I had done everything perfect, nothing could be better with it. This year, as I look back on it, on every page I see something I could do much better. I think this shows every person can improve, every day you learn something new.

Identifying Global Issues (Research)

Creating a quick scatter graph on the board, we graph the responses the kids bring in about the three top global issues. We don't end up with a clear majority, but our purpose was to take more of a survey than a vote. We explore why everyone doesn't agree and discuss whether consensus is necessary. We decide it isn't. Those groups who are ready share their charts and sing their anthems to the rest of us.

My kids read *Time for Kids*, a weekly newsmagazine that frequently has articles dealing with global issues. We have saved those issues and bring them out now. We also have e-mailed UNICEF for information on global issues, ranging from chronic persistent hunger to land mines, child labor, and women's rights (www.unicef.org). Now is the time for some thoughtful reading and thinking. The kids have also been collecting newspaper articles regarding issues. One of the related math assignments I gave them recently asked each student to read the front page of a daily newspaper for a week and then classify each article by whether it was local, regional, or global. Then they were to graph their findings, using a multiple bar or line graph. As one student said, "And I thought you had us do that because we were studying graphs in math!"

Another word for authentic in my classroom is *useful*. Connecting a math skill with social studies content is useful. Therefore, I believe the activity provides an authentic experience.

The family interview question is, "What if each country stood completely apart from every other country, so that no part of any country touched another? Would that make this world a better place? Why or why not?"

The Delphi Technique (React)

We discuss the family interview question. It's a perfect question for the human continuum. Those kids who think that if each country should be separated from the others stand at the north end of the classroom. Those who don't think this would improve the world head for the south end of the classroom. Those who are undecided stand in the middle of the room. Then we start the discussion. First, a volunteer from the north end of the room states his or her opinion. The opinion is answered by a volunteer from the south end of the room. Back and forth we go, until everyone at each end of the room gets an opportunity to state a position. Then the kids are given a chance to change positions. My hope is the that the middle-of-the-room kids will form an opinion and feel confident enough to commit to one position or the other. Checking with each group again, the kids have an opportunity to add additional thoughts, springboard off the opposition's ideas, and capitalize on strong arguments already shared. Students love this strategy, it is kinesthetic, personal, safe, and fun.

Now it's time for the students to select global issues to investigate and report on to the rest of the class. We refer back to the original list of global issues. We do not use the family graph as this needs to be the students' choice.

Deciding to use the Delphi technique, I ask each student to prioritize the five issues they think are the most important by giving the most important issue twenty-five points, the second most important issue twenty points, and so forth, and give the fifth issue five points. This technique will help us efficiently sort out the six or seven global issues that the children feel are the most critical in today's world as well as the ones they are most interested in.

Now, working in country groups, the students tally the points each issue earns. They list the top five issues identified by their group. Finally, each group shares their list of top five issues and the amount of points each issue has been given. Adding all the points

FIGURE 2–10 *Bryan and Andrew Discuss World Problems*

73

together, the final compilation identifies clearly the issues in order of importance as determined by students.

Each country group meets quietly to choose which issues they'd most like to investigate. If I feel we are pressed for time, I might put the top issues in a hat and have each group choose one randomly. The groups will have a few days to research an issue and develop a playlet to teach us about it.

Tonight's family interview question is, "The global issue my group is researching is _____. What are your thoughts about this problem?"

The Play's the Thing! (Represent)

The students research and practice playlets to teach the whole class about their particular global issue. In my classroom, playlets are very quick, very simple minidramas that: 1) identify the problem; 2) give some reasons for it; and 3) suggest some possible solutions. The energy and interest levels are high, and we are using bits of time throughout the day. I've learned to not give extended time periods for this kind of activity. Instead, ten- to fifteen-minute "focus sessions" in which the kids drop everything else seems to work well.

I notice some groups have decided to add graphics to their playlets. Some of the kids want to make a poster, illuminating their problem. Others want to make a chart listing "What Kids Can Do" to alleviate the problem. Others decide a graph would be a powerful aid to inform their audience. Tonight's family interview question is, "Will you join us for an international lunch tomorrow? Bring a dish to our potluck and we'll provide drinks, plates, and utensils. Come at 12:00 noon."

(Actually, I had informed the parents at the beginning of the unit that we would have this potluck lunch, so they had more than one day notice!)

Guests, Good Food, and Our Global Decisions (React)

The room is humming as we set it up in theater style. The families arrive and my students greet them, take their potluck item to the designated table area. Then the children show off their country map. When everyone has arrived and taken a seat, the students begin their presentations by introducing each newly created country and its characteristics, including singing the national anthems. Then they explain how they determined which global issues to investigate. Each group then presents their playlet and shares their possible solutions.

Next, my kids rearrange their chairs in a series of semicircles on the "stage" facing their guests while I remind them and their parents that the United Nations chooses a global issue every decade to which they dedicate their resources and energy. In the year 2000, it is time to choose a new issue. Turning to the children, I ask, "Of the seven issues presented here today, which one should be the center of attention as we start a new century, move to a new millennium?" The kids know there is no wrong answer.

The children discuss the seven issues. They use thoughtful phrases that reflect their understanding of point of view, such as "on the other hand," and "it seems to me." These kids have chosen to investigate child labor, AIDS, deforestation, refugees, air pollution, water pollution, and global warming. They decide, through thoughtful discussion, that the UN focus should be global warming. Their rationale? Deforestation plus air and water pollution are directly related to global warming. They conclude that if global warming isn't attended to, then it's very likely that human problems like refugees and child labor will be a moot point because people won't live here any more!

If you are a beginning teacher, you may want to try a modified approach. Do the mock United Nation activity, but practice it first. Give each student an opportunity to develop a stance and practice a position. You wouldn't need to rehearse the final outcome but you could go over the format and do some rehearsals so the kids are not scared silent. Encourage your students to think for themselves, to weigh evidence, and to listen thoughtfully. If your kids have been given opportunities to research and discuss the issues, if they have learned that they can risk sharing their thoughts without being teased or criticized, they will participate in this kind of activity. And if they aren't ready, don't conduct the final discussion in front of families. Instead, do it in your classroom with just you and the kids.

The international potluck is a huge success. I have more parents show up for lunch than I've ever had for an evening event. I think I've just learned something about the community I've taught in for twenty years! Tonight's family interview question is, "What did you think of our discussion? Did you agree or disagree? Why?"

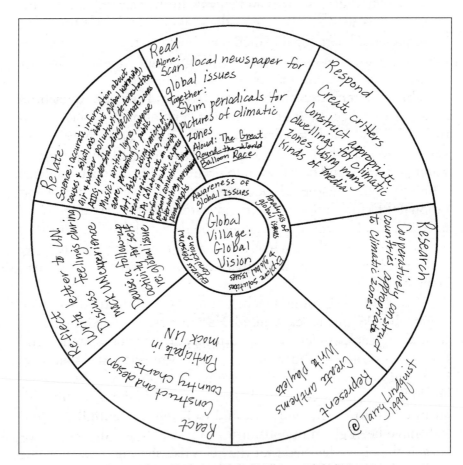

FIGURE 2-11 *Curriculum Disk for Global Village, Global Vision*

Becoming Active Global Citizens (Reflect)

After debriefing yesterday's incredible performance, the kids share their families' reactions: positive, incredulous, supportive. Everyone feels good about what we've accomplished. Now it's time for individual reflection. During the last few days of the unit each student writes a letter to the Secretary General of the United Nations telling him what he or she thinks the target issue for the next decade ought to be. (They don't have to choose the same issue the class agreed on yesterday.)

We have a quick review of business-letter format and the agreement that the letter contents should:

1. Identify the letter writer and the purpose of the letter.
2. Identify the problem.
3. Explain why the issue is important.
4. Identify possible solutions.
5. Urge the Secretary General to consider a particular suggestion.

Rough drafts are written, then final drafts completed. Although we may not have solved the problems of the world, we've given it our best shot! I then write a thank-you to the families for their support and have the kids share a copy of the letter they've written to the United Nations.

Making Connections (Relate)

Because the students had acquired a broad knowledge base during Windows on the World, the connections among disciplines and across disciplines are greater, more intense in this unit. Understanding the science involved, in several cases, became a critical factor. The kids needed to investigate and understand the causes and possible solutions regarding global warming, air and water pollution, deforestation, and AIDS. Some of this information tied into our health curriculum's goals and objectives. They also needed to understand the impact that weather and climate have on regions around the world.

Many of the students began to identify certain kinds of music

Part of this unit was making a country, something each group did and making a family out of walnut shells to live in that country. Each group got assigned a climatic zone (for example, we got tropical) and made our people and country according to what climate was assigned our group. I had a great time doing this. It was challenging, imaginational, and most of all, fun! I learned so much about world problems and how to get along . . .

List of materials needed for these units

walnuts (two or three per student); clay works as a substitute

marbles (one per student), optional

tempera paint, brushes

glue

googily eyes from craft store

bits of felt, yarn, feathers, craft "hair"

school milk cartons or individual cereal boxes

butcher paper

pieces of poster board or large tagboard for every four or five kids to share

access to nonfiction reference books and resources, newsmagazines, periodicals, newspapers, and Internet, if possible

Bibliography for WOW and Global Village

DURRELL, GERALD. 1987. *The Fantastic Flying Journey*. New York: Simon and Schuster.

Three children and their uncle fly around the world in a balloon to all seven continents and the four oceans. Facts and fantasy are blended in an appealing and unforgettable way. A great invitation to study world geography!

GAVIN, JAMILA. 1997. *Children Just Like Me: Our Favorite Stories*. New York: DK Publishing, Inc.

This picture book is a charming and informational collection of stories from around the globe. Universal themes are featured and real children introduce each tale. A thumbnail sketch of each child's life, environment, and culture is added.

HENNESSY, B. G. 1999. *The Once upon a Time Map Book*. Cambridge: Candlewick Press.

A delightful model for retelling any story by making a map of it. Students not only increase their map-reading and map-making skills, they also demonstrate what they know about what they've read. A creative and powerful model for integration.

KINDERSLEY, BARNABAS AND ANABEL. 1995. *Children Just Like Me*. New York: DK Publishing, Inc.

Created in association with UNICEF (United Nations Children's Fund), this book highlights the remarkable similarities and accents some of the differences among children and their lives around the world. Continent by continent, real children's lives are shared as well as geographic locations and features. This books provides a pattern that encourages kids to create their own page about themselves.

KRUPP, ROBIN RECTOR. 1992. *Let's Go Traveling*. New York: Morrow Junior Books.

Providing a model for student projects like Windows on the World, this book provides examples of the kinds of information kids might want to include as they explore different countries: locations and sites to see, maps, diary entries, important facts, short histories, vocabulary words, and a postcard.

MALAM, JOHN. 1996. *Highest, Longest, Deepest: An Exploration of the World's Most Fantastic Features*. New York: Simon & Schuster Books for Young Readers.

This picture book is made to involve and motivate young geographers. A foldout guide to the world's record breakers, it invites kids to find and create their own record-breaking page for local geographic features or those of a country or region that they are focusing on.

SCHUETT, STACEY. 1995. *Somewhere in the World Right Now*. New York: Alfred A. Knopf.

Take the mystery out of time zones while showing children the varied richness of the world they live in. Filled with lush paintings and a multitude of maps, the gentle text provides an engaging scaffold for helping students understand an important social studies and math concept.

SCULLARD, SUE. 1990. *The Great Round-the-World Balloon Race*. New York: Dutton Children's Books.

> Aunt Harriet and her nephew, William, and niece, Rebecca, enter a balloon race around the world. The race hits ten diverse countries, featuring geographical highlights. A good book to read aloud to the class before brainstorming the kinds of information kids might want to include in their research about various countries, regions, or continents.

MENZEL, PETER. 1994. *Material World: A Global Family Portrait*. San Francisco: Sierra Club.

> Sixteen of the world's foremost photographers traveled to thirty nations around the globe to live for a week with families that are statistically average for that nation. At the end of each visit, photographer and subjects collaborated on a remarkable family portrait, surrounded by their possessions. These photos vividly portray the look and feel of the human condition everywhere on earth. The same riveting data is available on CD-ROM as well.

Chapter Bibliography

BELLANCA, J. A., and R. FOGARTY. 1991. *Blueprints for Thinking in the Cooperative Classroom*, 2nd ed. Palantine, IL: IRI/Skylight Publishing, Inc.

ELBOW, PETER. 1973. *Writing Without Teachers*. New York: Oxford University Press.

FREEMAN, RUSSELL. 1987. *Lincoln: A Photobiography*. New York: Clarion Books.

FULWILER, TOBY. 1987. *The Journal Book*. Portsmouth, NH: Boynton/Cook.

GARDNER, HOWARD. 1999. *The Disciplined Mind: What All Students Should Understand*. New York: Simon & Schuster.

———. 1985. *Frames of Mind*. New York: Basic.

GRAVES, DONALD. 1994. *A Fresh Look at Writing*. Portsmouth, NH: Heinemann.

GREGORY, KRISTIANA. 1996. *The Winter of the Red Snow*. New York: Scholastic.

KEMPER, DAVE, RUTH NATHAN, and PATRICK SEBRANEK. 1995. *Writer's Express*. Wilmington, MA: D.C. Heath and Co.

LINDQUIST, TARRY. 1995. *Seeing the Whole Through Social Studies*. Portsmouth, NH: Heinemann.

ZEMELMAN, STEVEN, HARVEY DANIELS, and ARTHUR HYDE. 1998. *Best Practice: New Standards for Teaching and Learning in America's Schools*, 2nd ed. Portmouth, NH: Heinemann.

THREE

Doug's Unit: Immigration

Immigration is a unit that works well for upper-elementary and secondary classrooms. The curriculum for these grade levels usually includes some combination of community, regional or state history and geography, as well as a study of United States history. Immigration as the conceptual center of a unit suggests a number of questions that can lead to very productive experiences in the social studies classroom. Here is a short list of sample questions that are natural extensions of the concept of immigration:

Who lives in our community?

Where did they come from and when?

Why did they leave where they were before?

How did they travel? What did they bring with them, and what did they leave behind?

What was it like where they came from? What were their days like?

How is the place they are now similar to and different from the place they left?

What was happening elsewhere in the world as they were coming here?

Did they stop at other places on the way here?

How did they choose to come here?

How have they adjusted to changes?

How does our community meet the needs of its people, and how do our people contribute to the overall community?

What happens when different groups of people come together?

How do we learn about each other?

How do those who come to our community learn about us?

How do we develop rules and governance?

This is not a complete list of questions, and I would never pursue all of them. They suggest possible directions the work with your students could take, and they serve to help you plan the most effective journey you can make.

Some Things to Consider

Immigration is the family story of many members of your classroom. Be sensitive to this. First, some students who are immigrants are teased, shunned, or humiliated by others for a time after they have arrived, especially if they attend a school in which they are an obvious minority. Highlighting immigration as an issue may generate more of that kind of behavior. It should actually serve to eliminate prejudice in the long run (with knowledge and understanding gained through study), but there may be some tension along the way.

Second, the stories of families leaving their homeland for a new country are sometimes both powerful and painful for family members (including the students with whom you are working). These stories may call up life-threatening or difficult situations, time spent in refugee or relocation camps, friends and family members who died or who were left behind, or simple homesickness. Be supportive and sensitive to these possibilities, and allow for some alternative approaches to the assignment. Students who don't want to investigate their family's stories may choose the story of someone else from their country, or might choose to investigate the immigration story of people from an entirely different country, or from their own country at another point in its history.

Third, the events and history you know from the point of view of a United States citizen (and school teacher) may be known in very different ways by people who lived in the places where those events occurred. Be open to other points of view about situations with which you think you are familiar, especially controversial or partisan events. Students whose families lived in either Southeast Asia or Iraq, for example, might have strong opinions or perceptions about the Vietnam War or Gulf War (as they are called in the United States). It's important to check yourself for bias (and of course, to recognize that your students have their own biases and points of view as well).

Fourth, immigration is a thematic or conceptual center that could easily lead to months or years of study, in many different directions. The most significant challenge to teaching this unit may well be to limit the focus appropriately so that the experience is exciting, challenging, and attainable in the time you have available during the school year.

Parental Involvement

Send a note to the parents of all students, letting them know that you will be investigating immigration with your students. Tell them that you will be giving the students assignments to bring in family stories, about their lives in different places they have lived, and about their journey and adjustment to their current home. Ask for their cooperation and encourage them to call you at school if they have any concerns or questions. This note is important for two reasons. First, you don't want students or family members to experience the assignments as an intrusion into their personal lives. I always assure the students and their family members that we respect their right of privacy and will develop alternative assignments if required.

Second, you might find a wealth of information through family members to share with the students in your classroom. I have had parents come to talk about their experiences in Japanese internment camps and in refugee camps in southeast Asia. They all spoke of what their lives had been like in their countries of origin, what they left behind, and the adjustments they had to make in coming to the United States.

I also invite other members of the school community to add to our study of immigration. One year the star of our show was a janitor who had lived in Vietnam until the mid-1970s. He moved to Seattle to be with relatives (and to escape the communists) and has raised a family in the south end of Seattle. He came into class with pictures, stories, and insights about the entire immigration process and added greatly to all of our understandings of the experience. These interviews enrich the students' understanding of the process of immigration, afford them a look at some different places in the world, and change student attitudes toward the people with whom we have talked.

Possible Topics

Immigration is a unit that embraces many of the most significant and useful topics that your students can encounter, including:

citizenship	climatic change
"the other"	travel and trade
slavery	conflict resolution
economics	California's proposition 187, etc.
the law	indigenous people versus
class and socioeconomic status	newcomers
redlining and housing	stereotypes
the Holocaust	ghetto
identity	race
group membership	cooperation
individuals and states	personal responsibility
war	propaganda
scapegoating	manifest destiny

exploration	Chinese exclusion
Japanese internment	refugees
refugee camps	transportation
multinational business	labor issues
current class composition	school and community
changes in a place over time	places left behind
migrant labor	the Depression
unions	literature from around the world
folk art and customs	food
religions	governments
comparative geography	transportation
civics	

Select those issues or concepts of particular relevance to your class and situation and to work them into a unit that enhances the understanding, relevance, and skills of your students.

Integration

The unit that follows is a social studies-centered unit, but it is truly at the center of the entire school day in my classroom. The activities and sequence described reflect a "whole" day centered on the topic of immigration, although we are also engaged in various language arts, reading, arts, and science activities (we exchange students for math at my school so I do not include math in the unit).

I consciously focus on the central concept of immigration whenever possible. We are reading stories and novels about immigration in reading class, writing about immigration-related themes in language arts, working with the topic of immigration as we study grammar, spelling, and other language-arts activities. Our focus might be on paragraph structure, business letters, or subject and predicate; the content just happens to be about immigration.

We are also learning arts techniques that we apply to immigration-related themes, listening to music of various countries (related to places our class members and fictional characters have come from), working with photographs of immigrants, or of people involved in related situations (refugees from war, for example). We work with role-plays and other theater techniques to experience the difficulties of communicating with others. Again, these may be minilessons or techniques that appear in the middle of a lesson. They are a part of business as usual in the room, and so are not necessarily noted as specific integrating activities.

There are many ways in which curriculum can be integrated, and I try to do so whenever possible. I emphasize four aspects of integration in the immigration unit presented here:

1. An integrated curriculum centers on a central concept such as immigration. I have organized the unit that follows around this concept so that our language arts, reading, arts, and, to some extent, science work relate to it. We are learning the skills and content of those disciplines as well as broadening our understanding of the central theme.

2. An integrated curriculum can use the methodologies of one discipline to teach the concepts and skills of another. I make use of the language arts and arts disciplines to heighten the learning in social studies, for example. This approach is used throughout the immigration unit.

3. I strive to integrate the lives of the students with the course material. This is the most important aspect of the integrated curriculum to me, and it is the heart of this unit. I have started with the lives of my students and have built the curriculum around them. They bring in their family histories, stories, culture, and ways of seeing to the classroom.

4. Integration does not only mean working across disciplines; it also includes bringing all of the social studies (or language arts, etc.) subdisciplines together. Social studies is a wide-bodied discipline made up of several discrete disciplines.

It is essential to study them together rather than to attempt to understand any one of them in isolation. For example, you cannot understand the economics of a particular society if you don't understand their geography, their culture, their institutions, their history, or their relationship with their neighbors. Conversely, the geography of a place (past, present, and future) is intimately linked to the people who live there, the economic and political systems of the people, and the worldviews that they have developed.

5. There are aspects of an integrated curriculum that are not possible or relevant in my particular setting. I believe that it is most effective to present course material at the secondary level in a coordinated manner. If eleventh-grade social studies classes were studying the Depression years in the United States, for example, the language-arts classes could read the literature of the United States in the 1930s (*The Grapes of Wrath*, *Let Us Now Praise Famous Men*, and so forth). The students might listen to the music of the time ("Brother Can You Spare a Dime," "Life Is Just a Bowl of Cherries"), study the photographs of Dorothea Lange, and the works of artists hired through the Public Works Arts Project in their art classes. There were many different theater companies working on the federal payroll during this period, and the drama department might take on a play from this era. This integrated approach is not nearly so easy to accomplish at the secondary level as it is in elementary grades because it involves many teachers, classes, and curricula; but it *is* possible.

The unit that follows is so large that it could exceed a year's curriculum. I choose a path or sequence that makes most sense to me and to my students; I omit those lessons that are superfluous, or that simply don't fit, for whatever reasons. I encourage you to do the same.

Who Are We?

A number of exercises help identify who we are, and help the class to become a learning community. Begin the first lesson of the sequence by focusing on the geography related to the members of the class. We use a hanging map of the world and ask about where students have been: "Who has been to a country outside of the United States? Who has been to Asia?" It only takes a couple of questions to get things rolling, and the students are eagerly volunteering the places they have been. They might tell stories at this point, but it is equally valuable to save the stories for a later point, or for journal writing. Some of the students in the classroom may have only recently come to the United States, or to your city or town; the point is to recognize that most of us have come from somewhere else (either this generation, or their parents or grandparents). That is part of the human experience. I want to set a tone of acceptance (we are all members of this class who have gotten here by a variety of means, we all have our stories), and give a focus to learning the places and paths we have traveled through time.

This exercise can be extended to travel through the United States: "Who has been to Oregon? To Illinois?" Students raise their hands to indicate that they have been to the named states, reinforcing the idea that many of us have traveled to get to our classroom. The activity also helps to begin the learning process with regard to geography and map skills.

I sometimes have students trace possible routes between Illinois (or Vietnam) and Seattle. It emphasizes the neighboring states and countries and helps to focus students on using (and enjoying) maps. (*Note*: Since I teach in Seattle, this city and Washington state become the reference points for many of our exercises.)

Birthplaces

The next step is to have students locate the place they were born. This again can be done using a world map and pins or markers of various sorts marking the spots. Pins and thread allow all to see visually the path that got them from their starting places to their current places. Each student attaches a thread to the spot they started; use a pin or glob of sticky tack to make the attachment. Attach the thread from point to point as the student's family has moved across the globe until you reach your own city or town. The globe (or map) is quickly covered with multiple colored threads and gives further visibility to the paths we have traveled.

Parent/Guardian Place of Birth

This is a simple extension of the previous exercise, and is likely to produce a much wider range of data. Simply ask students to find out where their parents or guardians were born and to find those places on the map. Their locations can be noted with different colored markers if you wish (to differentiate from student birthplaces), but I don't usually make that choice as it gets too crowded (visually and physically).

The Place They Left Behind

Ask those students (and/or their adult family members) who are willing and able to share about the places they lived before to make a presentation about those places. This presentation can include photographs, stories, drawings and paintings, music, artifacts, and whatever else will help to describe the place. The focus is not on a big production, but on having students become more familiar with various places in the world.

First Day of School

Students recount their first day of school (at this current location). They might indicate what they had heard about the school (or you as teacher), what school they had come from, and what they were expecting. This can be done as a journal assignment, and can be presented in outline form so that students simply have to fill in the blanks, if that is most appropriate for your level. The form might look like this:

Name_____

When did you first come to this school?

Where were you before that?

What was it like where you were?

What was it like to leave that place to come here?

Did you know anything about this school before you came here? (What did you know?)

How did you feel before you came to school on the first day?

What was it like when you got here?

What did you notice early on the first day?

What things made you feel uncomfortable on that first day?

Were there things (or people) that helped you to feel comfortable?

What is the same and what is different about this place and the place you were before?

How do you feel in this school now?

Choose from the list of questions (and of course add/substitute your own questions); the idea is to allow your students the chance to reflect (in their journals, privately) about their experiences as new students, as new members to this community or classroom.

Have students share their responses with the whole group, and record the responses on the board (with no names attached), developing a class list of what it is like to come to a new place, and how we adjust to it. This exercise helps my students and me get to know who we are as a class and how we came to be together. It is a team-building exercise, geography lesson, social-skills lesson, and a chance for reflection all at the same time.

Stories

I believe that telling stories is an important activity for many reasons: It's fun, it's an opportunity for students to learn about speaking in front of others, it's a chance to learn about other cultures, it's a chance to practice learning how to be a good audience, it develops organizational and memory skills, it requires research, discipline, practice and risk, and it requires students to practice reading and rereading a text.

Early Stories

I love stories and believe that they are unparalleled learning tools. I ask students to bring in stories that they heard when they were very young. These stories could be folktales, favorite books, religious stories, creative efforts from a parent or guardian, or something else; the students choose ones they remember. I ask family members to come in and tell us stories whenever that is possible. It is especially rich when the adults tell stories in their first language first, and then retell them in English.

Students illustrate these stories, or tell them in cartoon-panel format (which includes both artwork and text). I have had arrangements with classes of younger students in which my students share their stories with the younger students, and that has often been wonderful; it does take some time to set up and to follow through, so you must decide if you have time.

Stories are one of the common elements to our being human; we all have them. We can investigate how our stories are similar, how they are different, and how they might have changed within a family over time.

Folktales

It is a logical next step to look at folktales from different cultures around the world. Include stories from the cultures represented in your classroom if at all possible. There are some basic questions to bring to the exploration of these stories:

Where does the story take place?

What is the setting like?

Who are the major characters in the story?

What is the basic plot?

What are the major themes or messages?

What is the problem or task?

What does the main character need to learn or do to solve the problem?

How does the story resolve itself?

What change does the main character go through?

How is this story similar or different from other stories read in class?

Telling Stories

Have students select stories from a particular country or culture; it can be their own or another. Their task is to memorize the story (or become very familiar with it) so that they can present it to the class. I encourage them to use a key-words sheet; they write down a list of words that will help them to remember what happens in the story. They may refer to this list when presenting their story; they may not simply read the story word-for-word from a piece of paper.

The key words for a story such as Red Riding Hood might look like the list on page 94.

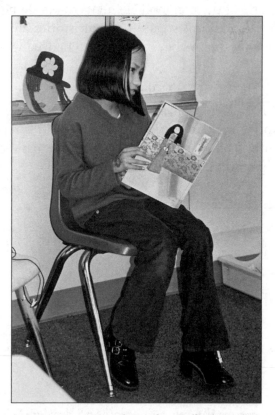

FIGURE 3–1 *Keneth Reads a Folktale to the Class*

Mother sends Red through the woods to Granny's

flowers off the path

wolf

wolf to Granny's house first

Granny in closet

big eyes, ears, teeth

woodcutter

This storytelling activity can be very simple and straightforward or can become a more concentrated unit, depending on the needs, interests, and ability levels of your students. I make sure that I read stories to mine every day. We practice identifying major characters, settings, plot lines, problems, tasks and knowledge the protagonists must attain, and the messages intended by the author. This is done with a light touch, but consistently.

We might take a familiar story and list the events in order, or I might scramble the events and have the students assemble them in correct order. They might present a familiar story in cartoon-panel form. They must present the basic events of the story in their sequenced storyboard, which means deciding on the major events, editing out lesser details that won't fit, and presenting the story in order.

The students prepare their stories and practice telling it to a variety of audiences, depending on their confidence levels and situations: a stuffed animal, or other inanimate object; a family member (if appropriate); a class member; and, if time permits, a small group of class members. When they have finished this sequence they are ready to present their stories to the entire class. The presentation to a small group is frequently omitted from my classes, but it can be useful for those who are nervous and working their way up to telling to the whole group.

I have found that some students take to this exercise and have their stories memorized in a day; others are less comfortable. Several students in my current class could only "tell" their folktales by reading them from the book. This was fine with me; they were gaining reading practice, experience in presenting material to their classmates, and they became familiar with the story. Some of these students were even comfortable reading their stories to other classes (not embarrassed at all that they had to use the book), and took pride and pleasure from doing so.

"Coming to Seattle" Stories

We collected "coming to Seattle" stories from all of the families in our classroom, and then from others in the school community. We asked parents, grandparents, uncles, aunts, or others to tell us the story of the first members of their family to come to Seattle. They described what it was like for their family members to live in their countries of origin, why they had to leave (or chose to leave), how they decided to come to Seattle, and what it was like for them to adjust to life in Seattle.

Students heard about families fleeing the Russian Revolution; the Nazis in Germany in the 1940s; war in Southeast Asia; poverty in China, Mexico, the Philippines; and discrimination in the southern United States. Our relatives came to Seattle to build the railroads, to work in the fishing industry, to raise money to support their families in China or Japan, or to raise their own families.

Students developed a list of questions, practiced interviewing each other, and then interviewed family members at home. Members from the school community (other teachers, instructional assistants, parents, grandparents of students in other classes) came to our class to share their "coming to Seattle" stories with us. Some were interviewed by the entire class, others by small groups. We recorded the interviews on tape recorders and asked adults to transcribe the interviews. The stories have now been collected into a book of approximately one hundred pages, including student illustrations. The book is kept in the school library, available for checkout. Each student also has his or her own copy of the book.

I sent letters home to explain the project and to begin the process of collecting stories. We received interviews from almost every family in the class; those students who for whatever reason could not collect family stories drew illustrations to accompany the interviews we had with members of the larger school community.

Here are excerpts from a couple of the interviews. Some are students speaking with relatives and others are interviews we conducted with members of the larger school community.

Deno

Q: Who is the first person in your family to come to Seattle?

A: No one in my family came first to Seattle because they all came together. My parents came from Laos in 1985 and we have been here for only 13 years.

Q: What was it like in Laos?

A: Over in Laos, every day you would hear birds and other animals. You see jungle everywhere around you when you live in a country. They eat rice, corn, and vegetables like they do in Seattle. In Laos it is very poor in the country. They eat meat only once in a while because they can't afford it. There were no music or TVs because they didn't have electricity. The houses were made out of bamboo and the roofs were made out of bamboo leaves. The people living there had to work every day, for example like getting food or walking to far places to catch water from the well. The only thing they did for fun was joking around and kids playing tag or climbing trees.

Q: Why did the family decide to leave Laos?

A: The reason they had to come here was that there was a war and they had to run away.

Q: Was it their decision to leave?

A: You had to leave or else you would die and there were no chances of staying.

Q: How did they travel?

A: The only way they could travel was on the plane. My parents stayed in San Francisco to transfer airplanes. They got money to ride airplanes from the government. It took them about one day to get here.

Q: Why did they come to Seattle?

A: Our uncle sponsored us to live in Seattle. That is why we came here.

Q: What was it like to adjust to living in Seattle?

A: The weather was one reason that they got used to living here. The environment was another one that they got used to. The hardest to adjust to was to understand the American culture. They had a hard time communicating with other people in Seattle.

Q: What is the best thing about living in Seattle?

A: The best thing about living in Seattle is they have more opportunity to look for a job and making more money. They could make a better career.

Q: What do they miss about Laos?

A: My mom missed her hometown and her pets. She wanted to see the banana and coconut trees in her town.

Q: Do your parents want to go back and visit?

A: Yes, they want to go back and visit, and even I do.

Q: How have their lives changed since moving to Seattle?

A: My mom's life changed a lot because she goes to school and gets degrees. She earns more money and she has a car. My mom doesn't have to work on a farm as hard as she always did. Seattle is a safer place for her.

Mr. O. (grandparent of a Kindergarten Student)

Q: Who was the first person in your family to come to Seattle?

A: I came with my parents. I had no siblings, so that was my whole family, my mother, my father, and me.

Q: Was your life good where you used to live?

A: Not very, and that's the reason we left. I was born in 1922, and in 1933, when I was eleven, the Nazi party took over and decided to persecute Jews. So we left in 1940, and those last seven years were not very good. That's the reason that we came to this country.

Q: When you left did you have to leave things behind?

A: We had to leave all of our money behind. When we left, each of us, the three people, were given three dollars apiece, and that's it. There was no money allowed for us to take out. Fortunately our trip was prepaid, not by us but by organizations in this country. All the train tickets and the tickets for the trip and the food that we consumed while we were staying at various places were

FIGURE 3–2 *Mr. Vu Is Interviewed About His "Coming to Seattle" from Vietnam*

all prepaid by somebody else. So when we came to this country, to Seattle, each of us had one dollar, and that was the total amount of money that we had. And all of our belongings, they were supposedly packed in a big crate and shipped, but the lift van was stuck in a city in Belgium when war broke out there was no way to get it through to this country. Whatever we had decided to ship was also lost.

Scottish Storyline

I usually begin a storyline sequence at this point in the unit, though there are times when I create characters as the very first step. Scottish Storyline is an approach to curriculum development and organization that is thematically based and that allows students to begin with their own conceptions of the topic of study and to come to knowledge through their own research and need to know. It is involving, challenging, and flexible in that students can enter at any level of sophistication and skill.

Scottish Storyline was brought to this country by Dr. Steve Bell and Dr. Ian Barr through the work of Dr. Margit McGuire, of Seattle University. They have introduced the process to teachers through workshops and teacher training, and through written materials (Dr. McGuire has published a series of units, called *Storypath*, with Every Day Learning Press).

Overview

Students create characters and a setting (time and place) out of paper. The characters' faces are defined by the unit theme; for this unit the students create the faces of immigrants. Two students work together to create one character; they decide on everything from the name, sex, age, race, and characteristics of the person to their favorite foods, movies, leisure activities, fears, and skills.

The class will also construct a mural or frieze of the location in which these characters live, including significant geographical and human-produced features. This setting for the storyline is created after students have researched the location, and serves as the basis for the events that happen.

The storyline process orchestrates a personalized and contextualized unit of study that helps the students to connect emotionally and intellectually to the course material. The next sections of this chapter will present a sample storyline outline on the theme of immigration. I hope it will serve as a model for teachers developing their own storylines, on topics that serve their students, curricular demands, and situations. Remember as you read this that storyline is a means, not an end. Use what is useful, modify as fits your situation, and omit what does not fit.

A Sample Storyline on the Theme of Immigration

Here is a storyline sequence focused on immigration. You will notice that some of the episodes or lessons are actually several steps in themselves, and might require multiple class periods to carry out. Evaluate the knowledge and skills your students already have and the skills required to carry out successfully the various tasks of the unit. Add those steps necessary to ensure the success of the students in completing the assignments. Common sense and your knowledge of your students are crucial to making this process work.

Let me mention here one of the essential rules of storyline: none of the created characters dies, ever. They may become sick or hurt, but they will survive the unit. This is not negotiable.

Creating the Immigrant Face

Create the face of an immigrant. Students work in pairs to create one face using "people paper" or other construction/art paper that gives a realistic range of skin tones to allow for many different racial and ethnic choices.

Working in pairs is important because it allows each student some distance from the character being created. If a student works alone in creating a character, it is riskier because he or she is more closely identified with the character's shortcomings. When students

Name_____ Students _____

Age _____ Height _____ Weight _____

Country of birth _____ Urban or rural _____

Birth family_____

Childhood memories _____

Favorite foods from original country _____

Favorite games or hobbies (in original country) _____

Parents' work _____

When did your character come to the U.S.? _____

Why did they choose to come? _____

How did they decide to come Seattle?_____

What did they leave behind? _____

How did they get to Seattle? _____

Did they stop anywhere on the way? _____

How long have they been in Seattle?_____

What do they miss most about their homeland? _____

What do they like most about being in Seattle? _____

Current family _____

What language(s) to they speak at home? _____

Pets _____

Current job or situation _____

Hopes _____

Fears _____

FIGURE 3–3   *Immigrant Biography*

FIGURE 3–4 *Deno and Steve Introduce Their Characters*

create characters in pairs, there is less one-to-one correspondence, and consequently more freedom to take risks. The paper face should be realistic in size. Students attach various face parts with glue sticks. The students must make decisions together about who the character is, what he or she looks like, and the details of his or her life.

Model the process by creating a face yourself, which you can display on a wall or board. Have the parts already cut out, but start with just the head shape and ask students what it needs to become a face. Add the eyes, nose, ears, mouth, and hair as class members suggest them. Attach the parts with sticky tack (or fun tack), a gumlike substance that holds well and does not damage walls. It can be purchased at most stationery stores. Have some fun with the process, suggesting various hairstyles or facial hair possibilities (full beard, mustache, mutton chops) so the students get the idea they can have fun with this. The emphasis is not on artistic excellence, but on the creation of their characters.

Develop a Biography

As students create the face they also develop a biography for this person. They must decide their character's name, sex, age, weight and height, and the answers to various questions such as those listed on the "biography" sheet on page 102. They will come by this information through discussion with each other and through the character of the person created.

The pairs of students stand in front of their classmates and introduce their immigrant characters. They answer as many of the biographical questions as they can, and may present their information straight off the biography sheet or in more conversational mode. You can allow for questions at this point (and might see the need to ask a couple of questions yourself to guide further work by the presenters), but also emphasize that the students have just met their characters today and may not know everything about them yet.

This process of character creation, compiling biographies, and presentation takes three to five days. I prefer not to have all characters introduced at once because it becomes too long for the students to sit. Those who finish slowly have time to catch up through the week as others are modeling the way of the work.

All of the characters are displayed together on a wall of the room and left up for the entire unit. They are best attached to the walls using sticky tack or fun tack.

Here are a couple of examples of character biographies:

Cris Taylor (Created by Deno and Steve)

Cris Taylor is eleven years old. He is five feet tall and weighs ninety-eight pounds. He is from Laos where he once lived with his dad and mom, his dog, and his parrot. He remembers his parents divorcing when he was young.

Cris and his dad came to Seattle from Laos about five years ago. They left Laos because it was boring there and because there was a civil war going on. They had to leave their nice home, their dog, and their parrot to come to Seattle. They knew a cousin who had visited Seattle and told them about it.

Cris and his dad flew straight to Seattle from Laos and have lived here ever since. Cris' dad works at Boeing and is happy he does not have to work so hard as he did in Laos. They are also happy that they have a nicer home than the one they left behind. They still miss that house and their dog and parrot, but they have a new dog, a cat, and a snake for pets.

Cris is currently going to school in Seattle. His favorite foods are pizza, nachos, chicken, rice, and beef. He likes to play Force Challenge. He also likes to collect baseball cards.

Cris is afraid of strangers and earthquakes. His main hope is that his mother will come back.

Maria Conces (Created by Kathryn and Veronica)

Maria Conces is a ten-year-old girl from Mexico. She is four feet, twelve inches, and weighs seventy-five pounds. She grew up on a farm in Mexico with her mom, dad, big sister, and baby brother. She remembers that once she got lost when she was young, on the farm.

Maria's family moved to Seattle about three years ago. They had to leave their farm because they needed more money. They came to Seattle because they heard it was beautiful and that there were jobs here. The family traveled to Seattle by boat. Maria was very sad to leave her dog behind.

Maria's parents now work at a jewelry store and they are happy that their kids can get a good education in Seattle. Maria likes to eat enchiladas and rice, and she likes to play on tire swings. She still misses her friends in Mexico and her dog, but she does like the schools and she has a new dog.

Maria loves to sing and sometimes sings in restaurants. She wishes that she could see her dog, and she wishes she and her family could be rich. Sometimes she is afraid that she might die.

Look at Demographics

The class looks at the demographics of the immigrant display: Who are your immigrants? Where do they come from? Why have they come to this country? How many men, women, children are in the display? How did they get to your location? Are they recent immigrants or have they been in your community for some time?

At some point you might investigate the most accurate current statistics for immigrants in the United States and in your community. How do they compare with your created characters? Reference librarians can be a great help in finding this information.

I did not specify any restrictions or guidelines about who these characters should be, or from what period in time. The students created characters who were all modern-day immigrants and who were children, approximately the age of my students. This is not what I had in mind when I started the unit, but it made perfect sense. The students created characters they knew best, who were like them. This changed the unit a bit since we did not have diversity in age or era, but it allowed us to focus more on the impact of place (how was it different to grow up during the same time in Vietnam, Mexico, France, or Seattle), and on the parallels between the lives of our characters and our own lives.

Apply Descriptive Words

Have students supply words that describe one or more of the immigrants. They can work first in small groups, or you can do this as a large group. Write each of the descriptive words on a small, white rectangle of paper and attach it to the wall surrounding the faces, creating a word bank. Do not attach any one descriptive word (*tired, bewildered, proud, strong*) to any face in particular, but encircle the faces with words. Do not allow sarcastic or teasing kinds of words; explain that these people are to be treated with respect. That does not mean that you can't use words that are thought of as negative (*lost, uncertain, dirty*) if they are truly descriptions that apply to one or more of the characters. These words will stay up with the faces, and students can make use of them as they write about the characters. Make sure they are large enough and dark enough to be seen.

Create a Frieze

Students create a frieze, or mural, out of paper, representing the place where their characters formerly lived. Ideally, this is one composite work that shows a location in which the characters "live." It is more complicated with this project since the characters come from different places (and perhaps time periods), but you can handle this in one of four ways.

If you are deciding to design the frieze, decide with your students what kinds of things need to be represented; divide the work, and have students create the frieze (drawing with crayons or markers on separate pieces of paper). You might create a basic intersection on one large piece of construction paper (one of those long rolls that are kept on dispensers). This gives the students a framework upon which to place various kinds of buildings, landscaping, ponds or fields, houses, stores, schools, and whatever else seems appropriate. Attach the individual drawings with sticky tack at the appropriate spot on the intersection. Make the pieces large enough (and dark enough) that they can be seen from anywhere in the room. Place the characters you have created on the frieze in a place they lived, worked, or played.

A second possibility is to have each pair of students create their own small frieze, representing the place their own character has come from. These can be displayed side by side, and class members can see what they have in common and how they are different.

Third, this step can be eliminated (for this particular storyline), and replaced by the model house exercise, described next. It is important that the students develop a clear sense of place, and both the frieze and the model house facilitate that sense.

Fourth, the frieze can be converted to a Windows on the World type project; students research the country from which their characters have immigrated and create a visual and written report. (See Tarry's description of this project on page 50.)

I chose to have my students make the model and the Windows on the World report instead of the frieze. It was too difficult to figure out the logistics of creating a unified frieze with so many different locations, and I was most concerned that the students get a strong sense of the place their characters had lived. I made the choice to combine the model and Windows on the World projects and was very happy with the results. The students enjoyed both, learned about the

FIGURE 3–5 *Thanh Shows Her "Window on the World"*

countries in different ways, had the opportunity to learn from each other, and felt successful about their work.

Construct a Model

Students work with the partner with whom they have created the character to construct a model of the place their character lived in before coming to Seattle. This is a research task as well as an art (model-building) project. Do this step whether you have decided to make the frieze or not.

Model House Project

I give my students the following instructions:

> The major part of this assignment is for you to construct a model of the building in which your character lived before he or

she left for the United States. This structure should be accurate in its basic shape and design. Make sure that your model is round if most of the houses in your character's hometown, city, or village were round. Make it look like it is made out of wood if they were made from wood. Make it look like it is made of bricks if the houses of that place are mostly made from bricks. You don't have to use the actual materials to make this model. You should find materials that are easy and safe to work with. You should also find materials that are very cheap to work with. Cereal boxes are a very good building material for this project. The boxes are easy to cut and to shape and they hold together with tape.

You are making a model of a house or building. It should be large enough to be seen easily. It should be light enough and small enough that you will be able to easily carry it to school and back home. We will be displaying our models for others to see, so do your best work.

We have gathered some books about the countries in which your characters used to live. These books will help you to find the information you need to build the model and to answer the questions.

You are also encouraged to get information from your own sources. You can talk with people who used to live in the country you are researching. You may use the Internet if you have access to that, or anything else that will help you to create the model.

This project is due on _____. That gives you two weeks, including two weekends. You will have some time during class, but you will also have to find time to work on this project outside of school.

I also give students questions to answer, to emphasize the connection among the climate, geography, topography, culture, and the kinds of houses that are built around the world. I want them to have fun building the models, but I also want them to learn about how things are connected in the world.

I bring in a range of school library books about living in various countries. We look through them, identifying the parts of the book that can be useful (table of contents, index, pictures, lists of illustrations and photos) in their research.

109

These questions will help you on your way to creating a model of your character's house in his or her country of origin (the place he or she lived before coming to the United States).

Your character's name _____ Student names _____

1. What country is your character from?
2. What is the average temperature in this country?
3. How hot does it get during the hottest time of year? When is this time?
4. How cold does it get during the coldest time of year? During what months does this occur?
5. How much rain or snow does it get? Is it spread out through the year or are there periods when it is very wet and periods when it is very dry?
6. What is the land like where your character lived? Is it in the mountains, near a river, near a desert, in the jungle or a forest? Is it a large city that used to be filled with trees or used to be a desert?
7. Did your character live near many people, or in a small town or village?
8. What were the houses made out of in this place?
9. Did those materials come from near the house or did they come from somewhere else?
10. Who built the house? Was it the people who lived in it or was it someone they hired?
11. How long did it take to build the house?
12. How long do they expect the house to last?
13. Who lived in the house? Was it one family, or one extended family (lots of cousins and aunts and uncles and grandparents)? Or many different families together?
14. Is there anything else we should know about this place where your character lived?

FIGURE 3–6 *Housing Project*

We visit the nearby public library in order to look through the stacks. I call ahead so that the librarian can gather relevant books on a cart for us, and we look through them, taking notes, making sketches, and problem solving.

Back in class, we collect cereal boxes and practice working with them. Cereal boxes are made of very thin cardboard and are easy to cut with school scissors. I teach the students how to open the boxes by running their fingers down a seam; the boxes tend to open flat and in one piece. I ask them to shape the cardboard into a closed, three-dimensional structure that does not use the fold lines of the previous shape, and to use masking tape to hold things in place. The object is to help students to become familiar with the cutting, taping, and shaping of cardboard, so the focus is on process rather than the object they form.

Then I have two student pairs combine their cardboard pieces into one collective shape. There is no requirement at any point that the shape be anything recognizable, or anything other than closed and three-dimensional. This gives them the chance to work with more cardboard and to collaborate with another group.

The students are free to choose the building materials for their model. Light cardboard is a good choice of material, but they can also choose other possibilities such as paper mache. I don't want them spending more than a dollar or two at most, and definitely do not allow prefabricated models.

I ask the students to present their work to their classmates, including their answers to the questions. We go through three or four presentations a day so that we don't get overwhelmed; the process also allows those working more slowly to be guided by the work of their classmates.

Reflection Sheets

The students fill out a reflection sheet after completion of the projects and presentations. I want them to consider their own work, the content of what they did, and their process. Many of the skills they learn during this project will be of use to them in later assignments. Here are the questions:

FIGURE 3–7 *David, Leung, and Jonathan with Their Model House*

1. What did I enjoy most about the project?
2. What was the most challenging thing about it?
3. What did I do that was most helpful?
4. What would I do differently next time?
5. What do I think was the best thing about my work?
6. What did I learn from this project?

The students had two major responses (to sum them up):

- The students enjoyed making the models and learning about the countries in which their characters had lived.
- They also learned a great deal about conducting research and about working in groups, which at times was challenging for them.

Two Days in a Life

Students create a story communicating a typical day for their character in their former country (or location), and perhaps a second story telling of a typical day in their new home. I describe the assignment as part of the storyline sequence, but it can also be taken on as an independent assignment related to the immigration theme. Students can research the countries their families have come from (rather than their characters' families), and then tell about a typical day in their own lives.

This assignment is simple conceptually, yet can be very challenging to complete. Students write a story of two days in the life of a person (who could be their storyline character); one day in his or her country of origin and another in his or her present location (or the time and place to which they immigrated). The story may be as simple or complex as they wish, but it must be accurate in its details. A contemporary of Abe Lincoln should not shut off his CD player in order to listen to the Lincoln–Douglas debates, nor should he or she listen to the debates on the radio while driving home from work.

This assignment can also be carried out on a smaller scale. You can have students write only one story, taking place either before or after immigration. They could also write the first story early in the process and return to write the postimmigration story later in the term. This makes the assignment a bit easier to approach, and the second writing will be guided by the experiences of the first composition.

Structure is very important to the success of this assignment. I begin by reading the children's story, *The Day of Ahmed's Secret*, by Florence Parry Heide and Judith Heide Gilliland (1990). It is a gentle story of a young boy in Cairo, Egypt who goes about his day delivering cooking oil to customers across the city. At the end of the day he reveals a secret to his family, that he has learned to write his name.

The story is simple but carries enormous amounts of information and required a great amount of information to create. The author communicates the sounds and smells and rhythms of Cairo, shows the architecture, range of employment, clothing, foods, and climate, modes of transportation, juxtaposition of old and modern, roles of boys and men (and by their absence, women), and much more in the course of describing Ahmed's rounds. When I read the story to a group of teachers, one of them who had spent time in Cairo was amazed at how clearly the author had communicated the city she knew.

After reading the story, the class compiles a list of what we know about Cairo from the story. We know, for example, that the city lies between a desert and a great river. We know there are cars and camels in Cairo. We know that there are oil sellers, rosewater peddlers, and various tradesmen on the streets, and that some children go to work at young ages, following the trades of their fathers. We know what some buildings look like, what people wear, and what we might hear and smell if we were standing on the street with Ahmed. The authors had to know these things in order to tell Ahmed's story.

I explain to the students that writing a story requires research in the same way that preparing to play a part in a play requires research. An actor comes to know her character in great detail in order to act in a convincing way. She knows what her character eats for breakfast, what she reads, what she watches on television (if she watches television or even has a television to watch), what makes her laugh or cry, what gets her angry, and what her favorite shirt looks like, even if those things don't appear in the play. It helps to make the character real for her so that she can "become" that person in a convincing manner on the stage or on film. A story author does the same with both place and people so they come across as true.

The students often look worried at this point and I reassure them that they are not yet professional actors or authors and that I simply expect as much detail as they can find. We then make a list of what the author of *Ahmed's Secret* had to know in order to write the story. The list usually includes (though often goes beyond):

what Cairo looks like (at least some sections of the city)

what it sounds like

what it smells like

what people wear

which people work and what they do

what it's like to be a young boy in Cairo

maybe what it is like to be a young girl in Cairo

temperatures and climate

family patterns and relationships

architecture (people walk up steps to deliver goods, lower ropes to deliver bread)

cultural and religious practices (telling time by the white-and-black thread at the end of the day comes out of the Muslim tradition)

what kind of streets (paved and unpaved)

which foods people eat and where they get them

cooking procedures

Students must decide what to communicate about the essence of a particular place and time. The students don't have to worry if another place sounds similar, since many places are similar; they should be concerned about communicating accurately what it is like to be in current-day Cairo, or eighteenth-century Paris, or eleventh-century Kyoto.

The students also decide how to communicate about their place. Ahmed's author does not say, "Cairo is a very warm place. The average temperature is thirty-three degrees." The heat is expressed through the types of clothing and buildings, the pace of Ahmed's rounds, the presence of the water seller. Having a character take time to lace up heavy boots, or to dampen a towel to wear around his neck might be a more effective means of communicating information than simply stating the temperature. The rule in theater and writing is to show, not tell.

The next step is for the students to identify the details they need to know in order to write their stories. They then develop plans for gathering the information. A list of possible sources of information includes:

relatives and/or other persons who have been in the place

encyclopedias (print and online)

novels set in the particular time and/or place

movies set in the particular time and/or place

paintings

documentaries

photographs

Internet resources

almanacs

Pictures are very useful in pursuit of this information. The students can find pictures of particular houses or structures from the time and place in question and can construct their character's day anchored to this particular place.

Students must decide how to evaluate the information they find in any of the sources, especially those such as novels, short stories, or movies, that are less bound by a requirement of faithful reproduction.

The students research their main character's town, and what his or her typical day is like. They might start by simply keeping an hour-by-hour log. Students might find it easier to record their initial ideas on a chart. Linking the process to the senses might also help to ground the experience, and to guide their research and writing. The chart could look something like this:

Time	Seen	Heard	Touched	Tasted	Smelled	Felt (emotions)
7:00 AM						
8:00 AM						
9:00 AM						
and so forth						

The final form of the work would look very different from this, but the chart can be of help as an organizer. They would be encouraged to have their character have at least three specific sensory experiences during each waking hour of the day, though all those experiences might not make it into the story.

The larger outline follows the character through his or her day. What does the character do? Does she light the stove; feed chickens; go outside to fetch water; run a long bath; turn on the television for aerobics; news; or cartoons; chop wood; tend to a herd; write a letter? What might he hear as he was doing one or more of those tasks? What would she smell? Would it be damp or dry? Would there be insects or icicles? What would he see as he looked out a door or window?

Details make the story work, but the challenge is to keep it simple: Ahmed has a very ordinary day. There is a slight tension in the device of the secret, but it does not cause him to leap from buildings or chase after thieves through a crowded market.

Students may complete this assignment alone or in pairs. I would also allow students to tell the story of a day in the place from which their own families immigrated, which might be of more meaning or interest to them.

A Day in the Life of Your Students

One step you can take to help your students get into the spirit of the day-in-the-life assignments is to ask students to treat themselves in the same way you are asking them to treat their characters. Have them document their typical day, perhaps using the same chart they are using as a first step for their fictional counterpart. They record their movements, what they see, hear, smell, whom they encounter, what they do. This will give them some support for taking on their imagined character's life in a more or less realistic way.

Presentation

There are several options for presentation. You can simply have students write the stories and hand them in to you. This can mean many papers to grade, but the assignment is clear and uniform. You can couple the above with the creation of a class book containing all stories that have been created. This book could be placed in the classroom, school library or even public library, with appropriate opening-night ceremonies. Students can create children's books, with pictures and only a few words of text. These texts could be shared with students in younger grades, at story times or as buddy readers. These stories could be turned into plays or readers- theater. They could be videotaped if you have the know-how and equipment. Students playing their characters from different times and places could interview each other about their lives, and compare and contrast their times and places. This could be done in a talk-show format or a more direct mutual interview. Characters could create poetry about their change in status. Prompts such as the following would help them to explore the changes they've been through:

I used to be_____, but now I am_____.

I used to_____, but now I_____.

I have_____, but I miss_____.

The first time I _____, _____happened.

Finally, the students could create clothing or costumes appropriate to the place and time of their story, create models of houses or other living structures, prepare foods, art in the manner and style, employ appropriate technology to do a task (churn butter, create a nailless wood joint, construct a suit of armor). Be creative and allow them to make suggestions you have not yet considered. Have fun with them.

Assessment

Assessment is a necessary part of any assignment, and there is both formal and informal assessment throughout this project. The biggest challenge throughout is to be very clear, with yourself and with your students, about what you are looking for. It is very easy to get side-tracked into the beauty or complications of the story and to forget that the larger focus is on research, on communicating factually accurate information about a time and place, and to understand about immigration. It is very possible to create a successful story that does none of those things, or to create a mediocre or poor story that is strong in many of those elements.

There are many small assignments within the larger framework of the story creation. Many of them look like more traditional assignments and can be graded as such. These might include map assignments (where is your place in the world), time line tasks (what has happened in your place before, during, and after your story takes place), country-information tasks (what does your country look like topographically, what do they produce, where are the lakes and rivers, and so forth). General research tasks can also be assessed traditionally.

The story itself is an opportunity to develop a rubric for this specific assignment. One possible rubric specifically designed for the assignment might look like this:

5	choosing an appropriate time/place
10	creating a list of appropriate questions for research
10	research strategies for answering questions
10	quality of research
10	story idea and realization
25	accuracy of information in story
10	quality of writing in story
20	link between life before and life after immigration
100	total

This breakdown of the project grade is a simplification. For instance, I would want to delineate what a 10-point "story idea and realization" looks like.

Another take on this is to not worry about an overall project grade, but to recognize that each of the discreet assignments that make up the overall project should be graded separately. This might mean twenty grades within the project structure, all independent per activity, but all within the scope of the story task. Rubrics might be appropriate for some tasks, not needed or relevant for others. That would be for each teacher and his or her students to decide.

Intoduce the Catalyst for Immigration

Introduce an incident that makes it clear that the characters and some or all of their family members must leave where they have been living for another country (or location). You might define the reason (earthquake, fire, volcano, political revolt, disease, crop failure, religious persecution, civil war) in a way that is historically accurate, or encourage students to research some reasons for their character's leaving. You can also leave it undefined since their characters come from different places and times.

Students must create a list of what their characters will take with them and what they will leave behind. They might have space requirements, and it must be historically accurate (no boom boxes on the *Mayflower*).

Students cut out the items they will bring (from paper) and place them in a paper lunch bag. It is most effective to have them cut out the items (rather than simply list their choices) since it is a hands-on activity that gives them time to talk with each other about choices. Students share their choices with the class; allow groups to make adjustments in their own bags when they see good ideas from other groups.

Investigate the Character's Journey to Their New Home

Investigate the mode of transportation to the new place. Why are the characters going where they are going; how will they get there; how much can they take with them? This may push students to reevaluate what they will bring with them. For example, if they are traveling by wagon, or on foot, they may have to leave the piano behind.

FIGURE 3–8 *LaToya and Rashonda Present Their "Packed Bag"*

Report on the Trip

Report on various stages of the trip. This could include journal entries, critical incidents (shipwrecks, illness, storms, friends who host characters through the winter), letters home, or letters sent on ahead to those awaiting their arrival. Some immigrants spent time in relocation or concentration camps. Handle this as seems most appropriate for your students and situation.

The New Location

A first look at the new location. What might immigrants have seen when they first came in to the harbor? This might be a place for a poem, a drawing, or other kind of artistic display. Here is an example, written by one of my students. It is based on a photograph of immigrants on a ship in New York Harbor in 1904:

Water, crowded people, the sky,
People's clothes, dusty floor, the cold air,
Babies crying, people yelling, the ship rumbling,
My last meal,
Dirty clothes, sea, the ship's equipment,
Happy, uncomfortable, nervous, ready to start a new life.

—*Deno*

Adjustment

What is the new place like? How is it similar to and how is it different from the place the immigrants left behind? What are they excited by in the new land? What do they miss about their former home? What changes must they make in their new home? This can be an artistic display, a written description, a letter to someone back home, a journal entry, a poem, or a skit. It does not have to be a major event, but it should be acknowledged in some way.

A Typical Day in the New Home

Create a story that tells of a typical day of the character in his or her new home. This is the second story described above in "two days in a life." Share the stories as presentations, or bind them into a book.

Prepare a Guide

A culminating activity might be to have the just arrived and settled immigrants prepare a guide for those who are to follow, helping them to be ready for the trip that they will soon be making.

This is one example of a storyline sequence; others lessons could be inserted to lengthen the unit, some could be eliminated to shorten it, and still others could be substituted to shift focus. The unit should be organized and carried out in a way that best meets your needs and the needs of your students as they learn the skills and content of their course curriculum.

Task Analysis

A task analysis is essential at each stage of this process. The questions involved in this process are both simple and general:

1. What do we already know about the topic?
2. What do we need to know and be able to do in order to carry out the task?
3. How will we learn what we need to learn?
4. How will we evaluate the accuracy and usefulness of what we are learning?
5. How will we use what we've learned to carry out the task?

The next step would be to identify potential sources of information: journals, novels, historical texts, encyclopedias, textbooks, movies, relatives or friends, songs, paintings, poems, and so forth. The students would track down the necessary information so their characters could pack for the trip.

This task analysis can and should be structured appropriately for you and your students. Scale the assignment to bring out what you want them to learn.

Sensory-Awareness Poems

Another step to take is a sensory-awareness poem structure that is very simple and can carry quite an emotional message. The students place their characters in a particular spot that is a part of their day. They then record, as that character, three things that they see, three that they hear, three that they touch, two or three that they smell, one or two that they taste, and two or three that they feel emotionally. The setup looks like this:

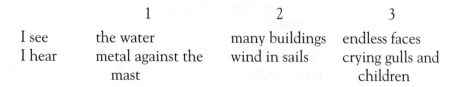

	1	2	3
I see	the water	many buildings	endless faces
I hear	metal against the mast	wind in sails	crying gulls and children

I smell   the sea   unwashed
I taste   bodies
I touch
I feel
  (emotionally)

    The grid is discarded, and what they have written in response to the prompts is read. It locates and defines a place and experience in a very powerful and efficient way.

    These two poems are based on a picture of a boy sitting in the midst of a bombed and burned city:

> Sadness, homeless people, collapsed buildings
> Crying, screaming, talking,
> Wood, moistness, dirt
> What used to be my home, pieces of wood,
> Dust in the air,
> I have no place in the world, sadness, and loneliness.
> —*Kristina*

> Nothing, fire, dead people,
> Fire, cracking wood, crying people,
> Smoke, blood, burning oil,
> Wood, dead bodies, fire,
> Flying wood, smoke, blood,
> Lonely, sad, already dead.
> —*Leung*

    These next poem is based on a photograph of a gang of immigrant children in an alley, in 1900's New York.

> Trash cans, water, and mud,
> Brick walls,
> People talking,
> Fish, dirty trash and a dead cat,
> Happy and mad.
> —*Tracy*

This last poem is based on a photograph of an immigrant family crowded into their kitchen, eating dinner:

My family, my food, my father,
My father speaking to my mother, my chair creaking, my little sibling crying.
A bad smell, dirt on the floor, my father who has not had a shower.
My slimy chair, my food, the table,
My food which I think is rotten, my bad breath, my father's bad breath,
Quite dirty, very hungry, stuck.

—*Leung*

Culminating Activity

The students come to this point in the immigration unit more highly aware of the challenges facing those who leave one place for another, no matter what the reason. They are particularly sensitive to those forced to learn a new language, new customs, and new ways of doing what had only recently been basic, daily activities. They are ready and eager to use what they have learned to make things a bit easier for those who come to the school, neighborhood, or city. The final project of the unit is to design and carry out an activity that helps newcomers to our area to feel welcome and to make adjustment to this next phase of their lives. I will briefly describe the general structure of the final project, pointing out possible variations that you and your students can choose.

Setup

We begin by reviewing what we have learned about ourselves and about the process of dealing with a new school, neighborhood, city, state, or country. We also review what we have learned about those things that make these transitions easier. The students share their own experiences of change, and identify what made things easier for them. We then brainstorm a list of things we could do to help students who are new to the school, new to the neighborhood, and new to the city. We then decide on a course of action and get to work.

School

The easiest and most relevant choice is to focus on the school community. Students brainstorm the kinds of things that make it hard to be in a new school, and develop plans for helping new students to feel comfortable and welcome. Students can form welcoming committees, buddy systems, create welcome-to-school booklets, and make sure that new students are invited to parties or activities. They can serve as guides and translators, especially those who have come from the same country, or who share a language.

It is fine if the plan is focused on the classroom or grade level rather than throughout the entire school. I think it is forcing the issue to expect older students to buddy consistently with younger students who are new to the school, and it is likely to be awkward for all involved. The students are often the best judges of how to welcome new classmates most effectively, and can take the lead gracefully and without fanfare. It is lovely when it happens, and makes a real difference.

You can certainly choose to do a larger action within the school, organizing schoolwide efforts. You must make sure you have the general backing of the school community, or at least the administration, and then coordinate the larger effort. It can be a rewarding activity, especially if done in cooperation with other classes who have taken a similar educational journey.

In Conclusion

A new student joined our class just before spring break, in mid-April of this year. The students and I talked about what we had learned about coming to a new place, about adjusting to a new situation, about the kinds of things that help people to feel comfortable and accepted. The students made several suggestions about what we could do to help make Cesar's transition to his "new neighborhood" easier and successful. We resolved to make sure he was included in games and activities. He has two classroom buddies who are checking in with him to make sure he knows where he is going around the building. In the first week, he was invited to two parties and included in the planning of an outing over spring break. He has a designated

FIGURE 3–9 *Class Members Have Welcomed Cesar to Our Community*

partner (who is fluent in Spanish and English) to make sure he understands assignments and classroom routines.

Cesar won't need these assists for long. He is a bright fifth grader who seems to be catching on quickly. It is significant to me that the members of the class were so ready to welcome Cesar to the classroom in ways that made sense to them. Their willingness and ability to bring him into the group quickly and naturally is evidence to me that they have learned some very important lessons from our study of immigration. They learned some information about the places and people living around the world, and they have become more familiar with the complex makeup of an American city like Seattle. They learned about why people move and what that process entails. They learned more about their own family histories, and about the diversity of experience and expertise that we have within our own classroom.

Equally important to me is that the students are now able to move beyond themselves and their own worldviews to understand the needs, concerns, and situation of others. They are translating that understanding into actions that make Cesar's move into our classroom as smooth as possible, for him and for all of us.

Unit Planning

Writing about unit planning is a bit like driving in a big city like Boston. There are too many things to pay attention to at the same time, and the roads are either one-way, or damaged. There are many factors seemingly designed to keep you from getting where you are going (traffic circles, construction, a river), and an attitude about it all.

Unit planning, like city driving, seems overwhelming at first, with too many things to think about and too little time to consider them adequately. As you make your first "short trips" into integrating curriculum, you gain the confidence, skills, and knowledge that will allow you to expand your range. It is a natural teaching act to link Lois Lowry's novel *Number the Stars*, which is set in occupied Denmark in 1943, and the historical reality in which it is set, as is situating the poetry of Langston Hughes within the Harlem Renaissance of the 1920s. Good teaching is making connections; you can't fully appreciate Langston Hughes, Sandra Cisneros, Lawrence Yep, or Bette Bao Lord's *In the Year of the Boar and Jackie Robinson* unless you know the social studies of their times and places. Conversely, these novels and poems can offer you and your students insights and information about the history you are studying. Your trips will lengthen, and you will drive to extraordinary places with your students. I will present an overview of my general planning process and then be more specific in presenting my process in planning the immigration unit that precedes this section.

My Fundamental Beliefs

There are certain fundamental beliefs that guide the choices I make when planning a unit of study. They are the bedrock upon which I layer the various skills, content, and themes of each unit. They reflect my strong bias toward both teaching children and to making sure that the content that I am teaching is meaningful and relevant to them. These are my fundamental goals:

- I want the students to understand the importance of point of view in our work, and to recognize that there is always more than one way of looking at things.
- I want the students to have a relationship to the course material, and for them to recognize the relevance of the material to their own lives.
- I want to take enough time to explore a topic in depth, and to help the students to learn how to take the learning process to topics of their own choice.
- I want the students to learn to conduct open-ended research, to conduct the research without prejudging what they will find.
- I want the students to learn material in context, to understand how the pieces fit together, how things affect each other, and how they are connected to the rest of the world.
- I want the students to be active, involved learners who are able to operate in many different modes and configurations (independently, in small groups, as a whole class).
- I want to make sure that each student has the chance to learn and succeed. This means that I will offer learning experiences that include and recognize the strengths of each learner, at least some of the time.
- I want to teach in a way that keeps me learning and growing.
- I want joy, and a passion for living and learning to be at the heart of the classroom.

So, planning a unit starts with these fundamental goals. I will design a unit that allows for students to be active learners, in a number of different modes: they will read, write, listen, design and carry out research. They will make use of a variety of arts media. They will work alone and as members of small groups. There will be at least one multistep project that requires the students to pull together what they know and what they have learned, hopefully about something that has interested them.

I also know that the focus of the unit will be on a theme that is complex enough to foster several points of view, that will lend itself to building and practicing the skills the students need to learn, and that will incorporate both the course content and student interests.

Finally, the unit will be one that invites us to invest our time, our energies, our interests, and our passions. It has to be about something that matters, to the students and to me. Ideally, it will be a unit that leads us to learn about ourselves and that moves us to take a real step in the world as social actors.

What Really Happens in the Planning Process?

Three or four things happen at once:

1. I look to see what is expected or required in terms of content and skills. Usually the requirements are pretty general, especially with regard to content. The content directives might say something like "Communities," or "Washington State History," or "World Geography." The assumption is that I (the teacher) will essentially follow the textbooks provided and everyone will be getting what they should get. There might be a laundry list of names, dates, and events to be covered, but no pretense of linking them together in any way, nor nearly enough time to do more than mention these names in order to check them off the list.

2. I am getting to know my students. I want to know who my students are; what they are interested in, what they have already learned, and what they can (and cannot) do. I involve them in a wide variety of experiences and assignments, initiate a number of discussions, present a range of readings, and spend time observing them so that I have some idea of who they are. If it is later in the

year (so that I do know them), I take time to consider what skills they still need to learn, and the things in which they are interested.

3. I take a glance through the assigned text to see what they are offering, noting chapter titles and major unit headings. I usually go through the assigned text (and perhaps one or two others) to make sure that I'm not likely to leave out anything essential. This reading serves as an overview rather than a search for specific facts or details.

4. I identify a central concept that will allow for a multidimensional study that can include several significant social studies themes. A significant concept at the center of a unit allows for students to study course content deeply, from many different points of view, and to come away with a much larger understanding of what they have encountered.

Concept-Centered Units

Here are three examples of concept-centered units that have been very successful at bringing students to significant learning:

1. Homelessness is a powerful entry into the study of communities. I want the students to redefine our assigned course content, communities, to include everyone rather than just the doctor, the lawyer, and the mayor. The concept of homelessness allows us to consider communities from many angles:

> Who are the people in a community?
>
> Why are some people homeless?
>
> What is/are the culture(s) of the people who live in this community, especially those who are homeless?
>
> How does this community define itself and how does it operate, especially in relation to those who are homeless?
>
> How do the members of the community relate to each other?
>
> What are the elements of power (what is it, who has it, why do they have it)?

How are communities similar and how are they different?

This central concept also allows us to take on a project that makes a difference in the world. I have taught this unit many times, and each time it has relevance to many of the students. Our school is close to a park in which homeless people hang out and sleep, and this is often a concern of students I teach.

2. Space is an effective central concept because it offers limitless possibilities for exploring social studies themes, literature, writing, science, and math. It also lends itself nicely to integrating the arts, especially theatre, visual arts, and music. Students map planets, make models of the solar system, design space suits and colonies, create a constitution, reenact Columbus meeting the Arawaks and Taino, calculate distances and times between planets, create stories and poems, and write books. Space is a versatile unit that reflects the interests of many students.

3. The unit included in this chapter focuses on the concept of immigration, particularly as it pertains to my current school, and to the Pacific Northwest. I am teaching in a community with a very diverse immigrant population. Most of the students are of Asian descent, some from China, some from Vietnam, others from Korea, Laos, the Philippines, or Indonesia. There are also African American students, an increasing number of Hispanics, and a few European Americans. It is a community that suggests an obvious question: Who lives in Seattle, Washington, and how (when and why) did we all get here?

Here is a brief list of some other possible concept-centered units. It is a small sample of an almost infinite range of possibilities.

democracy	change	shelter
work	childhood	food
cities	rural life	clothing
games	migration	endangered species
pollution	citizenship	religions
rivers	communication	problem solving

How Do I Plan for the Unit
Once I've Decided on a Central Concept?

There is an overarching, yearlong theme. An overarching theme can be as broad as Washington state history, the title of the course you are teaching, or it could be a theme that you are continuing throughout the year, such as the nature of power, or change, or contact with others.

Some of our students struggle with organizing and making sense of the many bits of information they have accumulated during the year. They will be more successful if we can help them to organize and make sense of what they have learned. Situating the current unit of study (immigration) within the larger framework of the course (Washington state history and geography) helps them to understand why they are learning what they are learning, and how it relates to other units of the course. We will refer to this immigration unit when we ride west with Marcus and Narcissa Whitman later in the year, to compare the experience of those who came from Asia to work on the railroads with those who came to Washington at other points in the state's history.

Each unit offers a mix of skills, content, and themes. I try to be as clear as possible with the students in identifying the skills, content, and themes that I want to cover in each unit. Skills refers to what I want my students to be able to do as part of their learning in the social studies. These skills include: reading for information from many kinds of texts; map reading and creating; getting information from a wide range of resources; communicating about what they have learned; using expository, narrative, and persuasive writing and speaking; and evaluating information for bias and accuracy. There is a list of social studies-related skills, as identified by the National Council for the Social Studies, in the appendix, but you can see from this list that we don't limit this consideration just to social studies skills. One of the principles of integration is that we can be meeting the goals and requirements of several disciplines within the same unit of study. We may also be considering the language arts, reading, art, math, and science skills we want our students to master as we plan the unit.

Content refers to the course material we want our students to know. This can include the facts and dates of the traditional social studies (where is Washington state, what major events have led to population shifts in the state, what kinds of work do people do). It can also include major issues and questions that arise from a study of the traditional content, such as "In what ways did United States business interests in South and Central America contribute to the devastation caused by hurricane Mitch in 1998?"

Themes are ongoing, larger questions that weave through the entire course of study. They become touchstones for each unit of study in that we will be comparing and contrasting how different people, at different times, have dealt with similar issues and needs. The National Council for the Social Studies has suggested ten themes or strands that lead to a powerful social studies program:

1. Culture: Who are we, how do we live our lives, who are other people, and how do they live their lives, and how do we deal with each other?

2. People, places, and the environment: Where do we live, how are we shaped by the places we live, and how do we affect the environments in which we live?

3. Time, continuity, and change: What is our story over time? Where have we come from, how did we get to here, and where are we headed?

4. Individual development and identity: Who are we as individuals, and how do we find our places as individuals and as members of the larger community?

5. Individuals, groups, and institutions: How do we, as individuals, function as members of various groups and institutions within society? How is society shaped by those various groups, including families, schools, religions, business systems, and the media? How do we, as individuals, shape our institutions?

6. Power, governance, and authority: What is power, who has it (and why), and how does that change over time? How do societies organize themselves, and how do they govern themselves? What happens to those without power?

134

7. Production, distribution, and consumption: How do societies generate what they need, how do they generate wealth, and how do they distribute that wealth to its members? Why is there a large income gap between those who own the production process and those who carry out the process?

8. Science, technology, and society: How does science and technology affect how we live, how we produce and consume, and how we view the world?

9. Global connections: How do societies see themselves within the world community, and in what ways do they make connections to that larger community? How does what happens in the United States change lives in countries around the world, and vice versa?

10. Civic ideals and practices: How do we live as members of a society? What does "right living" mean, and how do we function as productive citizens of a society?

These themes lead to a well-rounded, multifaceted study of course content, with attention paid to how they weave around and through each other. The guiding questions that arise from these themes are questions that direct students toward considering how different aspects of a society affect each other and the societies and lands around them. We might ask how geography affects the nature of power or wealth in a number of communities, comparing and contrasting what we find. We might look at various cultures around the world, comparing various institutions within them and trying to understand what they have in common. The latest scientific and technological breakthroughs have changed the way we live our lives, make our living, and how we live in relationship to the environment. The emphasis is on understanding how things are interrelated, how they fit together.

The various assignments and projects offered by the unit lead the students to develop and apply skills and content knowledge in increasingly complex and sophisticated ways. As the unit progresses, they will have opportunities to pull together what they have learned at earlier stages. They might learn the parts of a map in week two of a unit, for example, and need to create a map as members of an expedition in week six.

Units integrate across discipline areas as much as possible so that the students experience a coherent program as study. Students read and write about the unit themes in their reading and language-arts classes. They study relevant science topics when possible, and use art and music skills to carry out projects that tie in to the central theme.

Assessment as Part of the Planning Process

I assess the students (and the unit) constantly, through every means at my disposal. I am in constant dialogue with the students, asking them questions, discussing controversial or confusing issues, posing problems for them. I create readings that contain both content and a series of questions that allow me to assess for reading skills and for an understanding of the course content. Projects require research skills, synthesis of diverse information, and the ability to communicate that information to others. Tests, structured assignments, and a variety of experiences (creating maps, plays, trials, town meetings, papers, songs, and so forth) further enable me to assess how things are going (whether I need to fill in some gaps, move faster, enrich), and whether the students are making sense of our work together. I don't give the students a grade for the unit; rather I assess the various projects and assignments individually.

Assessment is a part of the planning process in that it helps me to know whether the students are mastering the material, whether they need more support in certain areas, or whether they are frustrated by the slow pace and ready to move more quickly. Assessment can also be a valuable component in directing my teaching; if I am expecting my students to be able to do certain things, I'd better make sure they can do those things.

A Specific Case: Immigration

Here is a brief description of how the immigration unit was developed.

I am teaching a fourth–fifth-grade classroom. This year our focus is on Washington state history and world geography. I looked through the Washington state textbook, looked back through my notes (I've taught this course before), and considered the students with whom I am working. There are ninety-two fourth–fifth grade students at Beacon Hill and five of them are European Americans. The students form a virtual United Nations, with representatives from virtually every continent, and at least a dozen different language groups, with Chinese being the largest.

I made a decision to study immigration for the first major unit of the year, a time when we are getting to know each other and are forming as a class community. I was new to the school and to the community and was looking for ways to focus on who we are. I used this study of immigration as a way of helping the students and me to know more about each other, and to help the students to understand the range of experiences and stories we each bring with us to the classroom.

The unit allows us to look at who we are as a class. The students will learn that virtually everyone living in our city comes from a family that originated somewhere else (or had to deal with the coming of others from elsewhere), and that our stories are different in some ways and similar in many others. I hope that this unit will be one upon which we can build the rest of the year's study. Each time we read about a group coming to the Pacific Northwest we will have some notion of why they came, what the process of coming to the northwest entails, and what the process of adjustment is like. We can compare and contrast it with our own experiences. My hope is that it will make that history a bit less distant; it will be something we share with all of those who came before.

I combined this information with the social studies strands suggested by the National Council for the Social Studies, and produced a list of possible guiding questions for the unit. I chose from this potentially endless list the following eighteen questions to serve as guides to the unit:

1. Who are we who live in Washington State?
2. Where did we come from, and what was it like there?

3. Why did we leave and come here?

4. What kinds of work did people do in their former locations?

5. How was that work related to the geography, climate, and topography?

6. What was it like to adjust to living in this part of the world?

7. What was the immigration experience like for those who were already here?

8. How did their lives change as others moved into the Pacific Northwest?

9. What kinds of work did immigrants do when they arrived in the Pacific Northwest, and what factors caused that to happen?

10. How are those jobs similar to or different from the work that people do today in the Pacific Northwest?

11. What are the crucial issues facing those who manage resources and work in the state?

12. What interests are involved and how are decisions made about what is good for the region?

13. How do people of various cultures live their lives?

14. How do people from different cultures get to know each other, and how do they learn to live with those from other groups?

15. Who are we specifically in this classroom and school?

16. How did our families come to this place, why did we come here, and what has our experience been like?

17. How do we deal with change?

18. How will this understanding of ourselves and of our community help us to understand the history of the region?

These questions shape the direction the unit takes, and help to define the larger choices of activities and projects.

I then made a list of the skills that students should master, or at least have some introduction to by the time they have completed fifth grade. I have used short descriptions, such as mapping, to include a range of skills and concepts:

mapping

group work

listening to others

reading for information from a variety of sources

storytelling

identifying bias

multiple points of view and perspectives

vocabulary

following directions

organizing, planning, and carrying out extended projects

presenting information

research

editing and communicating about what you've found through research

interviewing

writing in different modes, for different purposes

comparing and contrasting

decision making

reading and reporting about novels

linking stories to place

making links of various sorts of information

photography as a source of data

reading novels, short stories, and poetry

The list is long, and serves as strong input when planning the unit. I offered the students a range of experiences in the first couple of weeks so that they could show me who they were, what they were interested in, and what they knew.

With this information, I mapped out some possible pathways

through the course material, checking to see if these routes would ensure that my fundamental beliefs are met. The lessons of this immigration unit had to provide for active learning, focus on multiple points of view, offer the students the opportunity to conduct a research effort and to communicate about it, and offer a range of activities reflecting the learning styles and strengths of my students.

I began the unit with the Scottish Storyline sequence because it is relatively safe, especially at first, and it serves as a diagnostic for me; it helps me see both what the students know and how they are able to work with others. We researched the places from which these imaginary immigrants have come, built models of their homes (in their countries of origin), studied the geography and cultures of their countries of origin, and helped our characters to pack for the move to Seattle.

Then we studied ourselves. We collected "coming to Seattle" stories from our parents and grandparents. We then moved to the larger school community, collecting stories from students and teachers (and family members) throughout the school, which were combined into a book. This was done through a combination of whole-class interviews, written responses to a questionnaire we developed, and small-group interviews with parents at the school who were willing to share with us. Washington state governor Gary Locke (a graduate of this elementary school) sent his family story, and it was added to the others already collected. Students designed illustrations to accompany the family stories and the book is now sitting in the school library, available for checkout by anyone in the community. We charted the similarities and differences of the experiences that brought our interview subjects to this country, and noticed which items come up most frequently.

Finally, we brainstormed some strategies for welcoming new students to our school and community. These strategies were from a student point of view, and would help new students to feel comfortable as they joined the school.

We branched out and filled in, as needed, and the unit sequence fell into place. I chose novels to read that dealt with the themes of immigration, of moving, of dealing with those who are different, and of change (*Felita*; *The Iron Dragon Never Sleeps*; *The Monument*; *Number the Stars*; *In the Year of the Boar and Jackie Robinson*).

I checked to see that we were meeting both skills and content requirements, and designed activities to respond to those that had not been met, and also tried to meet the ongoing or emerging interests and excitement of the students. Our daily assignments reflected the overall unit theme, with spelling vocabulary, sentences designed for grammar learning and practice, reading practice (for comprehension), and journal writing, all focused on immigration-related topics. We took advantage of every opportunity to make connections and to reenforce learning.

I finally had to match this with materials available, either through the existing school supplies, my own "boxes o' stuff," and materials easily available through bookstores and libraries. I was not prepared to go deeply in debt in order to teach this unit, and had not taught it before. The school had some class sets of books that served as starting places, and there were wall maps of the world, the country, and the state. We made arrangements with the public library to carry out various research projects using their materials, both in the public library and at the school (they allowed us to check out many books on our topic). I used my classroom money (each teacher gets a small stipend to spend on the classroom) to buy some more books relevant to the topic, and some geography materials. Judi Slepyan, an extraordinary photographer whose pictures of the students light up this book, became a part of our classroom, and so we learned about "reading" photos.

Assessment

Students were assessed at several stages of the project. Here are a few points at which I assessed their work and behavior:

1. initial discussions about immigration
2. character creation and biography development
3. model-building project, research and development, creation of model, answer to questions
4. readings and questions on immigration

5. novels read (and questions answered)
6. letters to and from characters in other countries
7. interviews with parents and others
8. country reports, including map work
9. story creation (a day in the life)
10. poetry creation
11. various storyline projects (packing to leave, developing a set of questions and policy for immigration, town meeting participation on issue of immigration, advertising campaign for or against immigration, editorial cartoon on same topic)
12. school-based community service project
13. daily assignments in spelling, language arts, and art related to the immigration theme

The point of listing these here is to show that assessment of a concept-based unit is not simply one final grade to an overwhelming project. There are many assignments, and many of these are traditional in look and intention, and very easy to assess. The difference is that as many of the activities as possible fit into an overall, coherent unit.

Integrated Curriculum

I have made reference to integrating curriculum within the immigration unit itself, but want to expand on that a bit. A part of unit planning I integrate curriculum whenever possible, for three major reasons: 1) it is the way I already see the world (interconnected); 2) it means less work for me (planning lessons that bring together various disciplines and do double or triple duty, as reading, language arts, and social studies lessons, for example); and 3) it helps to reinforce what the students are learning throughout the day. Some of the integrated curriculum is obvious: We choose novels and nonfiction work that focus on the central concept of the unit, or we study the music or art that traveled with immigrants as they came to the United States.

Less visible integration occurs on a daily basis, as a matter of course. Lessons continually reflect the central concept (in this case, immigration), even when the focus is clearly on other disciplines. Students will learn their grammar lessons on sentences and paragraphs that have immigration-related topics for their content. We might or might not address that content as we try to identify topic sentences, or subjects and predicate, but the content is there, a given. Spelling words are chosen to fit with our reading lessons or research projects, and those are informed by the unit concept. When students learn to write letters, they are writing to real people who can help them to find out more about immigration, usually as part of a larger exercise.

This is not to say that every moment of the day is geared toward immigration. I do not force things to align artificially with the unit theme. I do take every opportunity that does fit to reinforce the learning that happens throughout the day.

This immigration unit offers many opportunities to integrate, within the social studies disciplines and across other disciplines. I rarely point this out to students (we're doing art now), but they are experiencing as coherent experience during their day as I can provide. I have isolated three areas of integration in the paragraphs below, to make this more explicit.

Language Arts

There is a growing list of stories and novels dealing with immigrant or migrant experiences. It is important to find stories that focus on the experience of as many different immigrant groups as possible, especially those groups represented in your school population. It is also important that the stories offer a somewhat balanced view of the transition, rather than a total fairy tale or propaganda piece painting one place as absolutely evil or hopeless and the other as the land of perfection.

We read a series of novels and nonfiction books about immigration, or about the challenges of moving to a new neighborhood, especially one in which the new arrival clearly stood out as different. We read books by Lawrence Yep, Jacob Lawrence, Julius Lester, Eve Bunting, Bette Bao Lord, Gary Paulson, Lois Lowry, Nicholasa Mohr, and Richard Freedman.

We read dozens of folktales from around the world, origin stories and *pourquois* stories (explaining how things came to be the way they are, like why there is rain or mosquitoes, or people of different colors and languages). We memorized folktales and told them to kindergarten and first-grade students. Currently, we are writing our own folktales.

We have read many books about immigrants in this country and stories about people coming through Ellis Island. There are many books of poetry about the immigrant experience, and we have read first-hand accounts of immigrant experience, shared through oral-history projects conducted with Puget Sound residents.

These stories can serve as read alouds (teacher reading to the whole class), and can also serve as texts for reading work, be it independent reading, reading groups, whole-class reading assignments, or as part of the research task.

Our immigrant novels and nonfiction books also served as the basis for our study of formal, language-arts skills. We used them to explore how authors created setting, described characters, employed literary techniques such as foreshadowing and mood. Using the same books for social studies and language arts helped the students to make sense of their learning, to understand that writing about real things also makes use of the skills of the language-arts discipline, and that these stories can serve as inspiration for the students' own writing.

We wrote letters and diaries as our immigrant characters, and stories about their days (as well as our own). We worked with a photographer to learn how to take and develop pictures, and how to "read" them. Our sensory-awareness poems (see page 123) are responses to photographs taken from the book *Immigrant Kids*, or from other books on immigration and war. We have also made photo documentaries about our typical days, and about things we care about, an alternative assignment to the day-in-the-life lesson (see page 113).

Spelling words came from the novels and nonfiction books that we were reading, from materials having to do with immigration and with living in other countries, and with words the students encountered as they investigated various aspects of their immigration work.

Drama

There are many opportunities for drama within an immigration unit. The topics of movement or change are the basic business of theater, as are the experiences of characters (historical and fictional) going through journeys (fictional, nonfictional, metaphorical).

Students can stage aspects of their reading, be it folktale, myth, legend, journal, historical account, primary source document, play, or other source. They can tell the story of the Israelites leaving Egypt, Native Americans waiting on shore as strangers appear, Africans being stolen and transported to the Americas, homeless children traveling by train to new families in the West during the mid-1800s.

Students can dramatize a particular event from a story they are reading that communicates an important issue or challenge relating to the character's struggle to remain in their country of origin, or their efforts to escape to a new country, or their efforts to adjust to a new location.

Students might present a readers-theater version of a traditional folktale, myth, or story, or could compile research into a readers-theater script, communicating what they have found through that vehicle. Readers theater is a form of theater that emphasizes text; there is no set, little costuming, and little movement. The actors sit or stand with their scripts in hand, and present the script to the audience.

Puppets, masks, costumes, and sets can enhance the presentations of stories and myths, but they are not essential. The point is to allow students a range of options for getting involved with and communicating about their research.

There is also value in "sub production experiences" that help students to appreciate the course content more deeply. I have students conduct small, spontaneous role-plays to emphasize points along the way. We played a game of Selwyn Says, for example (a very local version of the familiar Simon Says), but we played the game entirely in Spanish, and then in Hindi, led by students who spoke those languages. The students became very frustrated after a minute or so since they could not understand what to do. They had more compassion for those new immigrants who were essentially playing Selwyn Says in a foreign tongue for twenty-four hours a day upon their arrival in America. We also role-play asking for directions or other simple questions across the language barrier, and the students again experience the frustration that many immigrants would have experienced. These are small moments but they add to an appreciation of the magnitude of change associated with such a large move.

We spend a half an hour one morning speaking only Chinese. One of the instructional assistants leads the class, with pictures and gestures, and expects the students to follow her lead. Those who don't speak Chinese (the language of one out of every five or six people on the planet, and the most dominant of our school cultures) get very impatient and frustrated, though some manage to communicate across the language barrier through the pictures, gestures, and good will of the instructional assistant.

Theater can be a part of the research process in other ways. There may be plays or movies that show aspects of the immigration experience. This can be highly evocative and communicative, which also suggests some cautions. Make sure what is being communicated is accurate in its essential information, and make sure you talk with students about the "Hollywoodization" of history. I still remember Davy Crockett, Georgie Russell and the other stalwarts of the Alamo defending truth, justice, and the American way against the nasty, evil Mexicans who surrounded them. The truth of the matter is that Mr. Crockett and company were actually part of a war provoked by the United States in order to justify stealing land from Mexico, but that was not history according to Walt Disney. I did not learn the historically accurate story until a decade later.

Clothing itself can lead to extraordinary research experiences, and real learning about the immigrant experience. Tracing the creation of the clothing leads to virtually every aspect of the social studies discipline, from climate and geography through the economics and technology of the society, on through culture, roles, and family life, religious practices, and the process of change.

The style of clothing reflects the climate, level of technology, and economy of a region or area. It also reflects the values and morality of the people: Who wears what kinds of clothing, and in what kinds of situations? What is it that people do, and how does that influence their clothing choices? How are those decisions made? Are women veiled? What kinds of activities do the clothes allow and support?

The designs, colors, and composition of the clothing often communicate about the culture as well. Many cultures weave or paint in important symbols or figures of their culture as central elements of the design of the clothing.

Music

Music can also lead to an involved and productive investigation of the lives of the people you are studying. You can begin with the instruments themselves: What are they made from, where did those materials come from, what does that suggest about climate and geography, who made them? Who plays the instruments, how were they trained or selected, and when do they play? Is musician a label applied to a few, or does everyone take part? Is music for ceremonies only, or is it a part of the daily lives of ordinary citizens? What types of music are played, and what does it mean to the people of that culture (what are the songs about, who sings them, what attitude does the singer brings to the subject of the song)?

Bibliography for Immigration

ALTMAN, LINDA JACOBS, and ENRIQUE O. SANCHEZ. 1993. *Amelia's Road*. New York: Lee and Low Books.

This book deals with the challenges of migrant families coming to a community and leaving it. The main character, a young Latina girl, is looking for an anchor, some stability in a life full of change. She finds a tree she identifies with home, a place to which she can return. This knowledge helps her deal with the next move, and presumably, the one after that. The story works well in helping students process and deal with change in their classroom and their own lives.

AYERS, WILLIAM, and PATRICIA FORD, eds. 1996. *City Kids, City Teachers: Reports from the Front Row*. New York: New Press.

This collection of essays by an extraordinary group of educators emphasizes the voices and strengths of urban students. The reader begins to see the world from the many points of view presented in the text, and to hear the many voices of urban students and teachers as they live their lives in the midst of the inner cities of this country.

BELT, LYNDA, and REBECCA STOCKLEY. 1995. *Acting Through Improv: Improv Through Theatresports*. Seattle, WA: Thespis Productions.

The authors have pulled together acting and improvisation lessons from a number of master texts, and they have done it effectively. These lessons are adaptable for a range of grade levels and are explained well. I used many lessons to help students understand more about the experience of communicating without the benefit of language or common culture.

✶ BUNTING, EVE. 1998. *So Far from the Sea*. New York: Clarion.

This book follows a Japanese American family as they travel to an internment camp to say a final goodbye to the father/grandfather who is buried there. The book tells the story of the Japanese American internment of World War II, and the impact that experience has had on succeeding generations of Japanese Americans. The writing is strong, the illustrations powerful.

CHA, DIA. 1996. *Dia's Story Cloth: The Hmong People's Journey of Freedom*. New York: Lee and Low Books.

The Hmong people lived in villages in the highlands of Laos. They were drawn into the fighting during the Vietnam War, and many were forced from their homes. Dia's story is told in words and through Hmong needlework, story cloths that keep Hmong history alive and present. *Dia's Story Cloth* tells the story of Hmong families coming to refugee camps in Thailand, and then the United States. The book introduces students to the Hmong people, to the Vietnam War, and to the experience of immigration through words and incredible needlework.

✶ CISNEROS, SANDRA. 1991. *The House on Mango Street*. New York: Vintage.

Sandra Cisneros has written a book that is a series of connected short chapters from the point of view of a young Latina teenager. She and her family are dealing with living in a neighborhood filled with poverty, with ethnic diversity, and with strong emotions. The writing is very strong, and not entirely appropriate for elementary students, but several of the chapters are short and very effective at communicating the challenge of growing up in a changing world.

DAVIDSON, ART. 1994. *Endangered People.* San Francisco: Sierra Club Books.

Mr. Davidson uses text and vivid photographs to study endangered people around the world. He presents many different cultures and people who are at risk, for many different reasons. Some societies are seeing their centuries-old cultures changing, or disappearing under the pressures and influences of contact with the outside world. Other people are literally losing the land from under them, as the world moves to take over their place. This book is effective at highlighting some of the issues behind immigration and change.

FREEDMAN, RUSSELL. 1994. *Kids at Work: Lewis Hine and the Crusade Against Child Labor.* New York: Clarion Books.

Mr. Freedman looks at Lewis Hine and the work that he did in challenging the policy of using children as workers in the early 1900s. Mr. Hine made it his life's work to document the brutal treatment of child workers in hopes that he could change the practice, and Mr. Freedman presents his photographs and text in a very compelling format that generates much classroom conversation.

✳ ———. 1995. *Immigrant Kids.* New York: Puffin.

A photo documentary of the European immigrant experience around 1900, this book brings out different aspects of what it was like to be a child in an immigrant family new to New York and to the United States. The pictures present a visual historical record of the experience, and my class members responded to the kids in the pictures.

HEIDE, FLORENCE PARRY, and JUDITH HEIDE GILLILAND. 1990. *The Day of Ahmed's Secret.* New York: Scholastic.

This wonderful little book follows a young Cairo boy through his day at work in the city. The drawings and text communicate a great deal about the experience of living in Cairo, and about growing up. Ahmed's story serves as an example for having the students tell the story of their own days, and of having them investigate the ordinary lives of others around the world. It is a lovely story.

HEST, AMY. 1997. *When Jessie Came Across the Sea.* Cambridge, MA: Candlewick Press.

Jessie comes across the sea from her home village in the former Soviet Union. She is chosen to come when the village Rabbi decides he cannot leave his people to take advantage of a ticket that has been sent. Jessie deals with separation, with change, with adapting to a new culture and a new way of living. The book features beautiful illustrations and highlights the difficulties of learning to live in a new culture.

KNIGHT, MARGERY BURNS. 1992. *Talking Walls*. Gardiner, ME: Tilbury House.

Margery Burns Knight looks at walls around the world, from the Wailing Wall in Jerusalem to the Vietnam Wall in Washington, helping students to understand ways in which we are the same, and are dealing with similar issues and questions.

KRENSKY, STEPHEN. 1994. *The Iron Dragon Never Sleeps*. New York: Yearling/Bantam.

Stephen Krensky tells the story of the building of the railroad in California in the 1860s. The story is told from the point of view of a young girl (Caucasian), the daughter of a railroad executive. She discovers that much of the work on the railroad is being carried out by Chinese immigrants who are being underpaid and overworked. She befriends one of those workers, a boy her age, and is changed by the experience.

LAWLOR, VERONICA. 1995. *I Was Dreaming to Come to America: Memories from the Ellis Island Oral History Project*. New York: Puffin.

This book features both torn-paper collages and poetry to communicate stories of the immigrants who came through Ellis Island. These poems and art pieces communicate the pain, hope, and confusion of making such significant change under such difficult conditions.

LAWRENCE, JACOB. 1992. *The Great Migration*. New York: HarperCollins.

Jacob Lawrence's strong, stylized paintings tell the story of African Americans coming to the cities of the north from their rural homes in the south. The paintings are full of emotion and content, and show the changes people went through as they learned to live in the working-class cities of the Midwest and North in the 1930s.

LESTER, JULIUS, and ROD BROWN. 1998. *From Slave Ship to Freedom Road*. New York: Dial.

Incredibly powerful writing and artwork focus on the experience of enslaved Africans. The story begins with their travel across the ocean on slave ships, chained, follows them through auction, and on to plantations. It ends with their struggle to adjust to their new status as free men and women, with few skills and little experience in dealing with society as independent people. The writing and artwork is intense and some may find it too strong. I used it judiciously with my class and the students were very moved.

LORD, BETTE BAO. 1984. *In the Year of the Boar and Jackie Robinson*. New York: HarperTrophy.

This book follows Bandit, a young Chinese girl, from her family's home in China to her new home in Brooklyn, New York. Bandit must learn to adjust to her new home and society, as must her parents. At the same time, Jackie Robinson is breaking the color barrier in Major League Baseball, and the parallels are both obvious and painful.

MCKISSACK, PATRICIA, and FRANK MCKISSACK. 1994. *The Royal Kingdom of Ghana, Mali, and Songhay: Life in Medieval Africa*. New York: Henry Holt.

The McKissacks have written many books documenting the African American experience, and this one pays careful attention to the some of the places from which they came, emphasizing the sophistication, wealth, and culture of those early empires.

MENZEL, PETER. 1995. *Material World*. San Francisco: Sierra Club Books.

Peter Menzel and other photographers tell the story of economics and culture through pictures of families around the world. Each family is shown in front of their home with all of their possessions displayed. There is brief text, but the message is really in the photographs, and the book is a treasure in terms of comparing and contrasting how people live. There is also a CD.

MOHR, NICHOLASA. 1979, 1990. *Felita*. New York: Bantam.

Felita is a young Puerto Rican girl whose family moves to a new neighborhood. Her family is hoping they will find better schools and more opportunity, but what they find instead is prejudice and bigotry. Felita finds strength and wisdom in her family and friends, and recognizes the value of honesty and trust.

MOCHIZUKI, KEN, and DOM LEE. 1994. *Baseball Saved Us*. New York: Lee and Low Books.

———. 1995. *Heroes.* New York: Lee and Low Books.

Ken Mochizuki and Dom Lee have created picture books presenting aspects of the Japanese American experience around the time of World War II. They take us inside family life and inside the internment camps so that we know more about what it was like to be a Japanese American during the 1940s, and how that has affected succeeding Japanese Americans to this day.

NAMIOKA, LENSEY. 1995. *Yang the Third and Her Impossible Family.* New York: Bantam.

———. 1996. *Yang the Third and His Impossible Ear.* New York: Bantam.

The Yang stories follow a family of Chinese immigrants who now live in Seattle. The family is trying to adjust to life in the United States, and the books capture not only the obvious cultural struggles, but also the intergenerational ones. The children have to deal with pressures to fit in with their classmates, and are much faster to change than their parents.

OBERMAN, SHELDON. 1997. *The Always Prayer Shawl.* New York: Puffin.

This gentle story follows several generations of a Jewish family that comes to the United States. It is a study of how families both adapt and maintain their culture and traditions in new and unfamiliar surroundings. A prayer shawl representing the ongoing faith and tradition of the Jewish culture and religion is passed from generation to generation.

PALEY, VIVIAN. 1995. *Kwanzaa and Me.* Cambridge, MA: Harvard University Press.

Vivian Paley has written a powerful book based on her drive to understand and address real issues in her teaching. The book follows her questions about why her own school (and most others) are not successful in working with African American students. She speaks with former students, coworkers, and brings her own insights to the work. This book has helped me to work with students of different backgrounds and cultures, and to bring those kinds of questions to our classroom conversations.

PAULSON, GARY. 1991. *The Monument.* New York: Dell.

This novel is set in Kansas. A young girl (biracial and slightly crippled) is adopted by a family in Kansas and she struggles to learn about who she is, and about how to appreciate the world. She meets an artist hired by the town to create a monument, and he helps her to learn to see both others and herself. Paulson has written many children's books and has captured some very important elements of the struggle to fit in, and to appreciate oneself as unique and alive.

POLACCO, PATRICIA. 1992. *Mrs. Katz and Tush*. New York: Bantam Doubleday.

This book is one of a series of wonderful books by Patricia Polacco. Mrs. Katz is a widow who makes a strong connection with an African American family in her building. This is a very simple and wonderful story about how ordinary people are anything but ordinary. Polacco has written many books and they are all of the highest quality.

RETHINKING SCHOOLS. 1992. *Rethinking Columbus*. Milwaukee, WI: Rethinking Schools.

Rethinking Schools is a journal written and published by educators centered in Milwaukee. These teachers, and writers from around the country, are concerned with justice and equity in the public schools of this country, and they offer articles, resources, and narratives about issues concerning the experience of students and teachers in our public school systems. Many of their articles suggest lessons or discussion topics that I use in my classroom.

SELWYN, DOUGLAS. 1993. *Living History in the Classroom*. Tucson, AZ: Zephyr.

This book was intentionally aimed at a secondary school audience since arts-based teaching was virtually nonexistent at that level, but many of the lessons and techniques are appropriate for K–12. Lessons in the book are organized by art: theater, visual arts, media/commercials, music, literature and writing, and a brief chapter on the nature of history.

STANLEY, JERRY. 1992. *Children of the Dust Bowl*. New York: Crown.

Mr. Stanley tells the story of the Depression and Dust Bowl experience of the 1930s through photographs and text. It is a time in our country's history that the students know little about, and this book of photos and text will fill in some of the gaps. It also adds to the discussion of why people move, and their struggles to adjust when they do. It also blends nicely with lessons on photography and how they are also primary source documents.

———. 1994. *I Am an American: A True Story of Japanese Internment*. New York: Crown.

This is a picture and textbook and presents information about the Japanese internment experience. The photographs and text communicate about what it was like for the Japanese who were interned during

World War II. It is a serious book about a serious subject; the photographs are good and it is well written.

TUNNELL, MICHAEL O., and GEORGE W. CHILCOAT. 1996. *The Children of Topaz: The Story of a Japanese-American Internment Camp.* New York: Holiday House.

This book is built around a diary kept by a third-grade classroom at the Topaz Internment Camp. The book presents sections of the diary followed by commentary and historical information about the internment, and about the lives of Japanese Americans.

FOUR

Questions and Responses

Dear Reader,

This is not a chapter in the ordinary sense. There is no plot or storyline. However, you are the main character and we hope to provide some resolution to conflicts and problems you face daily in your classroom.

Please do not feel that you need to read this chapter from front to back. Think of it as a flip book rather than a novel. Look over the questions posed, and flip to those that most closely mirror your concerns and questions about teaching social studies. As you meander through the pages, we recommend you think back to our units to help you place our comments in an appropriate setting.

The questions are ones we have been asked at workshops, by teachers in schools, or have asked ourselves. These responses reflect our beliefs about how kids learn best and how we all can teach social studies better.

Sincerely yours,

Tarry and Doug

What Am I Supposed to Teach?

Doug's response: Teachers are often set up in their classrooms with little to guide them except the textbook and a vague syllabus that may consist of one word, such as *communities,* or *family,* or *neighborhoods.*

Some schools or districts offer more specific guidance about what is expected in the social studies classroom (or social studies portions of the elementary classroom), but the guidance varies greatly. In addition, the real guidance often comes from a veteran teacher down the hall, or from an educational leader in the school who spells out some specifics about what to teach, who offers to loan materials, and shares ideas and conversation about how he or she approaches the work.

This kind of support is often hard to come by as a new teacher, for many reasons. New teachers are often shy, reluctant to bother other teachers or admit to how little they know about what they are doing. Other teachers are busy and consumed by their own students and challenges, and may forget about the new teacher down the hall, especially once the year starts. Prep periods may not match up to encourage conversation, and they are so short, (with so much to accomplish), that it is not practical to communicate during those times. What to do? The state guidelines and individual district frameworks should offer guidance, at least in general terms, as to what should be taught; it is the purview of the teacher, students, and school community to decide on the specific course content.

One suggestion is to consider a thematic approach to content, as suggested by NCSS and others. This approach leads to a comprehensive, contextualized exploration of a topic, be it the westward movement of European Americans, the migration of rural populations to the cities, the changing neighborhoods of the 1990s, or the role of women in various societies and cultures. This approach allows you to teach the skills you want the students to acquire, provides specific course content you are required (or choose) to teach, and offers an organizing structure that encourages higher-level questioning and learning.

Paying attention to the skills and concepts you want students to have, you can make choices based on those items and their (and your) interests. If you are teaching neighborhoods, for example, you can be flexible about what aspects of neighborhoods you are exploring and how you approach the topic.

Where Do You Get Your Ideas?

Tarry's response: When I start thinking about a topic, ideas start to come to me. Maybe I'll piggyback on an idea I saw in an educational magazine like *Creative Classroom*. Perhaps I'll borrow an idea I saw hanging on a bulletin board in the hallway or dredge up a memory of something I did in school that made learning fun. I dust that idea off, refresh it for today's kids, and create a memory for my class. Talking to colleagues helps me find or refine ideas. Going to in-service training or taking classes often sparks ideas. Reading professional books and journals frequently guides my decision making. I have learned that I don't have to be original, but I do try to go beyond the text. Sometimes I use the teacher's manual but I usually try to come up a couple of alternatives before deciding how to teach a given concept or a certain theme. Also, the Internet provides many lesson-plan ideas and possibilities for structuring a unit of study.

What Materials Are There for Teaching Social Studies at the Center?

Doug's response: Lots. The first step is to redefine textual materials as more than a textbook; way more than a textbook. These materials range from obvious social studies stuff like maps, globes, atlases, and other geography artifacts. Historical novels, plays, poems, artwork (paintings, sculpture, quilts), period clothing and furniture, music and musical instruments, cooking implements and cookbooks, stamps and letters, journals and newspapers are all social studies textual materials. The Internet provides so many materials that it is both daunting and liberating. Videos can be wonderfully useful, either in short, select segments (illustrating a time or place, raising an issue) or as complete films. The point is to consider what you want the students to learn and experience in the classroom and decide the materials that will help you do so in the most interesting, involving way possible.

157

How Do I Start a Unit?

Tarry's response: Social studies units can begin in many ways. For example, some teachers find a piece of literature that connects to the theme in some way and read it aloud to their classes. Others find a song, a poem, or a piece of artwork that invites kids to ask questions or wonder about the concept. Sometimes, I use a newspaper or magazine article to stimulate interest. One successful strategy is to show a product made by last year's class and encourage the kids to talk about it. Inviting in a guest speaker or going to an assembly, performance, or on a field trip often creates questions and invites comments. CD-ROMs or Internet sites can begin research. Try simulating an activity, such as shopping in colonial America, to spur questions and tap knowledge. Revisit the activity at the end of the unit to see what the kids have learned.

Some teachers find the KWL chart helpful. *K* stands for "what I know," *W* stands for "what do I want to know," and *L* stands for "what did I learn?" This strategy often works likes this:

1. Identify the topic, using a chart for the whole class or notebook paper for individual responses.
2. Write "What I know" at the top of the chart or page and ask the kids to respond. List their responses. You will find out what your kids already know or what they think they know.
3. Then write "What do I want to know?" Ask the kids to respond and list their responses. We find this part of the KWL process a bit "teacher heavy." Kids often don't know what they want to know. It has been my experience that the kids generate much better and more student-centered questions after they've had an opportunity to do a bit of reading and research.
4. Collect individual papers or keep the chart to bring closure to the unit as the students list "What I learned" later. My kids often respond to this task in their reflective assessment, the final activity that brings a unit's study to a close.

I think the most important thing about starting a unit is getting the kids hooked on the concept or theme. Find the most engaging, attention getting, stimulating opener you can and proceed from there.

Doug's response: I agree with what Tarry said, and would add that the students often give me ideas about what units to teach and/or how best to begin a unit of study. I try to connect my skills and content objectives to their interests and passions, and sometimes there are some obvious connections. I began my first unit on homelessness in response to student concerns about some men who were sleeping in a park near our school. I had wanted to explore community in an engaging and inclusive manner and the students provided us with an entry point.

What If Neither the Kids nor I Know Anything About the Topic?

Doug's response: This is often the case with first-year teaching assignments, and can seem overwhelming, especially at higher, more content-heavy grades. There are several ways you can approach this situation.

It is possible to model the process of approaching new material with your students. How do I, as an adult learner, approach learning about something new? What do I need to know? What questions do I have? What have I heard about this place or event and from where? What possible research choices are there? How do I evaluate them?

The question now becomes, "How do we approach what we are investigating?" The teacher can learn with the students. This approach, guided by the teacher's experience in investigating topics in the past, will help students to learn the content through learning the skills of the social studies.

It is important that the teacher stay ahead of the students in that he or she must be able to decide how to proceed from a timing point of view. You must know enough about a topic to be able to steer or guide usefully, but you don't have to be an expert. You can do your research as the students are doing theirs, and you will move at a faster pace so that you have some idea of what is likely to surface and to be

159

able to make plans accordingly. This might include locating speakers, field trips, experiments, paintings, or something else that will enhance the study of the topic. You can do this as you go, and part of your efforts can serve as discussion points or examples of research to share with the students.

You can also work with your librarian (school or public) and other resource people who can help locate materials and websites. They can help to gather a cart full of books on a topic that you can bring to your classroom or to a section of the library so that you can read them and so your students can carry out their projects. They can make suggestions about people you might talk with, videos you might preview, museums or facilities you might visit, or other sources of information or insight about the topic.

How Do I Encourage Passion—My Own and My Students'—for Topics?

Doug's response: First, allow your passions into your room. Are you passionate about gardens, animals, music, baseball, opera, railroads, theater, history, literacy? All of these can offer you and the students a way into a study of the world. You know about these topics, you probably have materials and connections, and you can communicate your excitement because it is real.

Students also have things they care about passionately, and these can often be used to help them learn "school stuff." I learned long division as a child through figuring batting averages and earned-run average for the local baseball teams (and my little league teams). I did this on my own time, for my own reasons, but the learning stayed with me because it mattered to me and I was willing to work at it. Use every opportunity to shape your curriculum and strategies to include the interests and enthusiasms of your students.

How Do You Foster Student Inquiry?

Doug's response: The simplest and most direct response to this question is two-fold. First, give the students the opportunity to ask questions and to research topics in which they have a real interest. Second, listen with real attention to what they have to say, while ensuring that their classmates do the same. Students have their own interests, even at those times when they seem to show little interest in your choice of topics. I have my best success in teaching them the skills and process of inquiry by allowing their interests to guide their research paths. Students can learn just as much about how to "do" inquiry by researching baseball or a favorite musician as they can with a more academic social studies topic. I feel comfortable moving them and their newly learned skills toward the required course content as a next step in the sequence.

I am also most successful in helping students to learn the inquiry process when I take their interests and efforts seriously. That does not mean that I accept what they say automatically, but rather that I listen carefully and offer careful, honest responses and guidance so that they feel both encouraged and challenged at an appropriate level.

Tarry's response: Fostering student inquiry can be very basic. For example, consider starting a unit of study by asking the kids to list everything they've ever wanted to know about . . . the West, Native Americans, pioneers, the Civil War, the Constitution, colonial life, Canada, or ancient Greece. Create a long list of questions. Most of the kids' questions will be factual in nature: who, what, where, when. Some will be a little higher level: why, explain, how. Decide if you want to push the kids gently to get some higher-level concerns listed: "If you were a founding father . . . ," "What would have happened if Lincoln . . . ," or if you want to, wait and add some thoughtful evaluation and supposition-style questions later. If you can find one of those handy little paperback books whose title is like, *If You Lived in Colonial Times* (Ann McGovern) or *If You Were There When . . . Time,* you can get a good idea as to the kind of answers your kids need to be finding. Don't be shy. Add one or two questions that interest you. Or add one or two that you know are important to understanding the topic and the kids have missed.

After listing all the questions, have the class help you place them into categories. For example, a study of pioneers moving west might break down into native peoples, reasons for leaving, getting ready, trail life, emergencies and unexpected events, making a new home. Ask the kids to choose which category they want to pursue. Usually there will be three or four kids working on several questions within a category. Give them a time limit to complete their investigation and choices about how to present their findings to the class. Give them time to do the assignment in class so you can monitor and assist. Encourage the students to use multiple resources. Teach them how to use the index to quickly scan for information. Keep the classroom moderately quiet so reading and thinking can occur. Work with the small groups on plans of action so each member understands his or her responsibility and agrees to certain deadlines. This is, of course, an ongoing, extended lesson. It may take a week or more to accomplish. Part of unit planning is the flexibility you have to determine how much time is needed for each lesson. Your estimates of when activities need to be completed will be based on your observations (are the children busily engaged or starting to mess around), your resources (are there alternatives available), your time (is a long vacation coming up or a field trip planned that the kids need prepared for), and your sense of timing (like good theater, there are always moments in a unit when it's time to move on).

How Do I Learn to Listen to My Students?

Doug's response: This may be the most important question of the entire section and one of the more difficult questions to answer. One step is to be sincere about wanting to hear what your students have to say. I try to ask questions that are real (I really want to know the answers), and then take the time to listen to the student responses. I insist that other students be quiet when their classmates are talking, acknowledging that they may not be listening but they may not interfere with those who are trying to listen.

Listening is a multilayered activity that includes what is said, how it is said, what was not said, how it was not said, the feelings within me when hearing what has been said, the actual content of the communication, and the responses of the students to what has been said.

Students come to trust your interest and your fairness, which tends to generate more openness and response. They notice when you allow their voices to enter the room, and tend to use them more. They learn to listen to each other in ways that you model and demand.

The most essential elements of listening to students are safety and respect. Students must know that they can be safe in saying what they have to say, without fear of put-downs, reprisals, or other consequences, from the teacher or their classmates. They must also feel that what they say has value and is treated with respect and consideration. There is room for people in the room to make mistakes, to exhibit thinking in progress, and to change their minds as they gain information and arguments from their study.

Where's the Textbook?

Doug's response: We both use trade books, research texts, picture books, novels, biographies, historical fiction, first-person accounts, primary-source documents, maps, journals, magazines, resources in our communities (including, especially, our classroom and school parents and family members) to assist in our studies.

We use the textbook sparingly, for several reasons. First, most textbooks are brief, surface presentations of events that may or may not be related. Second, the writing style is often dry and unappealing to students. Third, textbooks often reduce rich, multifaceted issues to simple, safe summaries, which rarely inspire the students to want to know more, because they have come to care about what they are learning. Primary-source documents, novels, newspaper accounts, and passionate, opinionated statements about a topic or issue are more likely to engage the students' hearts and minds, and to invite them to wrestle with the complexity of the world. We want to help students to live in this complex world, so look for materials to communicate this state. Fourth, we would rather have our students learn to use the tools of the real world, both because they have more useful information, and because they are more likely to support a love of research and exploration. Fifth, textbooks are expensive. We believe that a school's dollars could be spent on resources that deliver more value.

The primary concern of textbook companies is book sales. They want their product to appeal to as many districts as possible, and do not want to risk alienating potential buyers by including challenging or controversial viewpoints. These decisions may make sense from a business point of view, but they do not necessarily lead to a quality social studies program. It is important that the teacher makes use of the textbook in a way that serves the educational program that she or he has developed, rather than allowing the textbook to be the curriculum.

We would choose to have a teacher's guide to the text (to make sure we are covering the bases), and a few of copies of the text so that the students can make use of them for research purposes. We spend the rest of our resources on those books and materials that will make the most difference in our classrooms.

Do I Cover Everything in the Text or Can I Choose Fewer Topics to Do In-Depth?

Doug's response: Social studies is often one of the least popular classes in surveys done on such matters because it is often presented as simply a collection of unrelated facts, dates, battles, people, and other stuff to memorize. There is little meaning to be made, and the students come away with little insight and little to show for their efforts except a grade of some kind, and a distaste for the subject. There is no way to teach everything; it's pointless and painful to try. It makes more sense to consider what is most important for students to learn about their world (and the course content), and to involve them in an active, interesting, and thorough study of those things. They learn in a way that helps them to make sense of what they are investigating, to understand the diverse and varying points of view that lead to particular decisions being made.

It is important to understand what is expected of you as a teacher of a particular grade level. Are you expected to cover U.S. history through Reconstruction, or World War II? Are you dealing with topics like communities and families, which are more locally focused and less linked to what students study in later grades? Are you covering state history or geography, in which it is assumed you will cover certain basic skills, concepts, and content?

Part of the strategy, as noted before, requires a conversation with the social studies (or elementary) teams, to be clear about what is happening at different grade levels. The state guidelines and most district plans are emphasizing more teaching for depth and understanding and less teaching to check off a long laundry list of facts, but it is important to be clear about what is expected. It is also your responsibility to add your voice to the conversation, emphasizing what you think is important and what you want to emphasize. The team must decide how to cover the social studies program over the K–5 experience.

What Materials Support a Nontextbook Approach?

Doug's response: This is a topic that becomes more clear as you gather experience with the students and the topic, which is small comfort during your first year of teaching. There are hundreds of trade books that link particular topics; the NCSS list of notable trade books is one place to start. This list is released every April and identifies about one hundred books by theme and NCSS standard that are accurate to the culture or historical period, sensitive to ethnic issues, and worthy of reading. Annual, single copies are available for $2.00 and a stamped, self-addressed envelop from The Children's Book Council, 568 Broadway, Suite 404, New York, NY 10012. The Internet has websites and discussion groups that offer a variety of opportunities for approaching topics.

Biographies and historical fiction can be good jump-off points for study (see Chapter 5), or a means for organizing an approach to an era or concept. Textbooks do have value in these studies, but as sources of information, much like an encyclopedia. It is crucial that the textbooks serve your approach rather than the other way around, and it becomes clear that you do not need a class set of textbooks to teach in this manner. If allowed, try using textbook money to purchase maps and globes, magazines, and trade books.

How Can I Coordinate with Others?

Doug's response: Coordinating with others can seem like an overwhelming task, especially when you are new to a school or to teaching, and it is something that usually happens slowly. But this coordination is well worth the effort. There are four reasons why coordination with others makes good sense:

1. You have the opportunity to exchange points of view and feedback about the units you are planning and teaching. Having a second, supportive eye on your work is invaluable in helping you to make what you offer most effective.
2. You know things that your partner does not know, and vice versa. You can maximize what you bring to your students when you are working with someone else because you are collectively wiser.
3. You can plan and teach smarter and more effectively by dividing the work load between or among members of a team.
4. Teaching is a very isolating activity. It is very easy to lose your perspective when you are alone in a room with twenty or thirty children, and that is not healthy. It is especially dangerous if things are not going well (and there are days, or weeks, when it won't be going well; it happens to all of us). Talking with peers can make a significant difference. You can vent to a friend, which is often a very useful first step toward improving your teaching life. You can talk through possible strategies you might employ to address things that are not working in your room. And you might find that you are not the only one who is going through what you are going through, which can be very reassuring.

Begin your collaborative efforts with those teachers with whom you share some connection, some common interest. Don't worry about working with everyone, or with anyone on all things. Just pick some possible overlaps and work with someone in your building. You might coordinate one lesson, or activity, with an art or music teacher, or with a colleague teaching the same grade level. You might coordinate with a parent of a student in your room who has both interest in and knowledge of a topic, or with a colleague at another school studying the same or related topic. Or have your older students read with younger students in another classroom.

For example, your students might create a map of the known world at the time of Columbus' voyages for students in another room reading *Morning Girl,* a novel by Michael Dorris. Or classes might write letters back and forth, as they or others make imaginary wagon train trips, or fly through space, or live on the streets. Coordination can also take place through team conferences at various points, to decide on direction and resources. It is an opportunity for the more senior teachers to make suggestions and recommendations about materials and themes, with young teachers contributing as they are able.

Some staffs choose to make use of their regular meeting times to form study groups. Teachers with common curricular interests carry out their own, focused study of relevant literature and research. Each teacher is expected to choose a topic of interest, and every other week is devoted to the groups, alternating with the whole staff meetings focusing on schoolwide issues and business.

You might also decide to collaborate with teachers at other schools. You might have regular meetings, to compare notes and ideas, or you might develop a phone or e-mail exchange. Someone outside the building gives you a window on the teaching world you may not have within your building, and affords you a relatively safe ear for debriefing your experiences.

Where Can I Find Support for Creating an Integrated Curriculum?

Doug's response: This is an important question. You can start by identifying one aspect of your curriculum that you would like to know more about, and locating one or more others in your building (or network of friends and colleagues outside of your building) who will study it with you. You can decide on certain books to read, or ways to research the topic, meet on a somewhat regular basis to discuss content, strategies, or various aspects of the topic, and move on from there. It does not have to get official approval, need not cost anything, and doesn't have to meet someone else's schedule.

The thought of more meetings is a bit unattractive, but when you are working on a topic of your choice, with people who are interested, the time will be valuable and enjoyable. You are making the choice to do this. It is fine to aim small, to research a manageable aspect of your work, and your focus can be on something you can bring to your classroom in the short term.

Tarry's response: There are certainly workshops and more formal classes and opportunities available through school districts and at local colleges and universities. They usually cost money and require a time commitment, but are often worthwhile. One of the downsides of teaching at the elementary level is that you can lose the stimulation of dialogue with other adults about intellectually challenging topics. College classes or workshops can sometimes give you that stimulation, and can help you to make contact with others who are interested and excited by the same topic. These classes can also offer support through both materials and ideas for your classroom. Consider making the initial investment of time and energy to take classes that look interesting to you. Go toward your interest rather than toward classes you feel you should take, because those "shoulds" can be deadening to your enthusiasm.

Internet, teaching cohorts, study groups, pursuing what you are interested in, working with others who value this approach, asking questions, joining professional organizations are all steps you can take toward integration.

How Do I Talk with Administrators and Parents About This Approach?

Doug's response: Administrators and parents want to have a clear sense that you are approaching your work knowledgeably, carefully, and respectfully. They want to know that you are paying attention to the state, district, and school requirements, that you are paying attention to the students, and that you are thoughtful about your work.

Administrators and parents can relax if you show them how your approach will meet the standards your state and district have developed. Be specific in showing how the thematic approach to teaching will be meeting those standards. As you travel into space and your astronauts are mapping planets they will be meeting state standard XX; as they vote on a common set of rules they will follow, they are meeting civics guideline 00; and as they write letters from space they will be meeting communications standard YY. You can help administrators and parents to see that you are meeting the requirements of your teaching.

What About Standards?

Tarry and Doug's response: Not to worry. If we do a good, thorough job of designing and teaching social studies the students will more than meet the state or district standards. We design units in ways that make the most sense, informed by our students, the particular content with which we are working, and the skills we want our students to have and to hone. We teach in ways that maximize understanding, active learning, and involvement. The students do learn facts, but only in pursuit of higher-level knowledge. We do use the standards and district frameworks to double-check our design, to make sure we have covered what is important to us.

The irony is that there are very few standards for what makes a standard. There are various examples created by national, state, and local groups, but they do not collectively offer a unified vision of what constitutes successful social studies teaching and learning. Many states demand discreet, discipline-based benchmarks at the same time that districts within those states are encouraging their teachers to integrate the material and to teach thematically. It is a real challenge to a teacher to meet such conflicting demands. State social studies councils share concerns about how many state standards often aim at the lowest common denominator. They do not

FIGURE 4–1 *Putting the World Together*

offer guidance or leadership toward quality social studies, but rather present the teachers with a false sense that their most minimal efforts produce an adequate social studies curriculum.

In response to the standards, we simply teach as well as we can, involving the students emotionally and intellectually. Units such as the ones presented in this book meet the social studies standards of virtually every sort.

How Can I Teach Well When I Am Expected to Meet State and District Assessment Requirements That Are Not Based on Thematic, Integrated Social Studies?

Doug's response: If you deliver good social studies classes you will be meeting the district and state guidelines. It makes good sense to become familiar with the state, district, and school guidelines and standards for three reasons: you will know what is expected of you; you can communicate effectively and thoughtfully with your administrators and parents about those standards and how you are meeting them; and you can allow yourself to relax since you are meeting virtually all of the standards by offering a good social studies program.

Tarry's response: Good teaching pays off! Kids who have had plenty of experience reading from many different sources and who have the opportunity to think critically about issues do well on social studies tests. Kids who have had several experiences writing from different points of view, who have constructed Venn diagrams, and who can compare and contrast events, times, or people do well on social studies tests. Kids who have fun during social studies class usually do well on social studies assessments.

What About Testing?

Tarry's response: I always think of tests as a learning opportunity rather than a final judgment. There are times in our lives when we have to master a specific body of information and prove that we remember it (like our first driver's test), so I think it is important to practice that skill. That's what testing mostly is in my classroom, practice. My kids practice matching, short essay, expository writing, listing, and open-book tests on occasion. But the tests are not at the end of the unit. Tests are fun, a challenge, a personal best, not the end of the world, definitely not the only measure of student learning during a unit.

Assessment in my social studies classroom, on the other hand, consists of teacher observation, student products, and student performance based on rubrics constructed by me or by the children and me. It is a collection of "snapshots" of each student throughout the unit. Each snapshot captures the student using a different intelligence, practicing a skill, utilizing a concept, and working with others. These academic and behavioral snapshots inform me and allow me to frame vignettes about each student as a classroom citizen, a learner, a leader, and a follower that I can share with the student and with his or her parents.

Doug's response: I rarely if ever use testing in my classroom except to test for very basic information, like spelling or math facts. I do occasionally have students design their own test questions or activities as we move through a unit. They are directed to prepare a question that they think would get at the heart of what we have been studying, and we spend time talking about the questions as a class. The questions are often very insightful, and the activity helps the students and me to assess their learning.

How Do I Assess Nontext or Nontest Work?

Doug's response: There are many ways to assess, and this is a crucial question in the current climate. First, we already are assessing what goes on all the time, every minute of the day. We notice what is working, what is not; whether we need to move faster or slower. We may decide to go back and fill in some background information or to broaden our presentation to enrich it. We might turn some of our students loose to work on their own while we spend more time with others. This is assessment: It happens constantly and often doesn't get recognized as real assessment because it doesn't always get written down in the grade book; but it is actually the most authentic assessment we do.

Second, each of the projects or lesson sequences within a concept-centered unit comes with many subparts. Many of these individual parts are educational activities that are assessed easily using traditional methods. Students read and/or research for information in service to the larger projects. They have to organize information, write letters, papers, journals, and opinion pieces, calculate distances, diameters, and days until the oxygen runs out if they are in a space capsule or submarine, create maps, and many other easily assessable tasks as pieces of the large project. The overall design of the thematic or conceptual unit organizes the various educational experiences into a meaningful, connected sequence. Each of the activities can be assessed or graded, and students can be held accountable for each piece.

Students can also be assessed according to rubrics that they and the teacher help to develop. They would decide what an excellent piece of work looks like, and what it must contain in order to be successful. Rubrics can be very useful tools in both demystifying the grading process, and in helping to define a task so that students are clear about what to do.

Rubrics are not the answer to every assessment challenge and we find that they are best used sparingly, and carefully. They do take time and everyone in the room will be quickly sick of them if you try to create rubrics for everything. Pick a couple of key assignments throughout the year and develop rubrics for them.

How Can I Do Projects and Still Meet Grading Requirements?

Tarry's response: Break the project down into its components. Let's say the kids are doing a three-week project on U.S. presidents. One of the things they do first is search for resources, read biographies of presidents, and take notes of significant events. You could set up a rubric that requires a minimum of three resources, requires the kids to have read their biography by a certain date, and requires a certain amount of note taking in specified areas. You could end up with three assessments (or grades) from this part of the project.

Now, let's assume that the kids have to do something with their notes. Perhaps they have to create a picture biography storyboard. Create another rubric that requires certain organization (must identify president, tell about his life as a child, reveal problems he had to overcome, and identify main accomplishments), details (accurate information, must list resources used in proper bibliographic form), and quality (storyboard must be in color, attractive, and original). There are three more potential grades.

Taking it another step, now let's have the kids share what they've learned from the president project with another class. Set up the requirements for an oral presentation. Invite the kids to help set the criteria: Speak so everyone can hear, make eye contact, know your stuff, get our attention, end with a bang. Bingo! One more possible grade.

How Do You Get Community
Members to Come into Your Classroom?

Doug's response: I am happily surprised at how members of the community are willing to come into classrooms to share their interests, stories about their jobs, their childhoods, their pets, their music. It can make a huge difference in how your students feel about what they are doing.

When my class studied homelessness, we invited a counselor from a drop-in center for homeless teenagers, and a couple of those homeless teenagers. They told their stories, answered questions, and the slightly fantastic pictures that my third graders had created were clearly changed by the experience. We also invited the mayor (who came to talk about the city's response to homelessness, and to take back suggestions my students had come up with), and an administrator who ran an emergency apartment house for families. All of these guests added immensely to our study of the topic.

When we created quilts for a class of homeless students there were many parent volunteers who were able to help us with the sewing and cutting. One parent supervised the entire operation (being a quilter herself), and others put in many hours of crucial time. The quilts came out very well, and a local television station sent a reporter to do a story on their work. The students told of their trials and tribulations with the quilts, and their reasons for making them—to help kids who don't have homes or beds—and they were on the news. The topic kept getting more and more real, more and more exciting as we brought the world into our study.

When we studied newscasts and commercials we invited members of some local television stations to visit with us, and two of them did so. Again, it made our study much more real and exciting. They talked about what happened in a television newscast, brought video samples of various aspects of their work, and helped the students with the stories they were practicing. We had a chance to watch the local newscast from the studio, and we toured the station and then watched the noon news.

Our subsequent newscast was a far cry from those professional efforts, but the experience of meeting professionals in the field made the students much more conscious of their work, of various aspects of the tasks, and of a desire to do things well. It enriched the study immensely.

Should I Use Documentaries in My Classroom?

Doug's response: This is a wonderful tool to use in the classroom, and there are some steps you can take to maximize its effectiveness. There are some basic questions one should use with documentaries, including an awareness of who is financing the film, who is making the film, the reasons they are making it, as well as hidden points of view. I have a list of fifteen questions I use with my students when we view a documentary:

What is a documentary?

How is it different from a feature film?

What is the subject?

Who is telling the story?

What is their point of view?

How are they expressing the point of view?

What supporting evidence is there for what they are saying?

What are other points of view represented in the film?

What are they *not* saying and who is *not* represented in the film?

What questions do you have about what has been raised in the film?

Who funded the film?

What bias and/or prior knowledge do you (as audience) bring to the film?

In what context are you seeing the film?

When was the documentary made? In what ways might that affect what has been said (and not said)?

Why was the documentary made?

Are Feature Films Useful in
the Social Studies Classroom?

Doug's response: Movie studios have created their own version of history. Walt Disney's version of Davy Crockett at the Alamo, circa 1950s, defined the history of the Mexican American War for many people, much as the movie *Pocahontas* defines early contact between Europeans and Native Americans in the 1990s. This means that many students (and adults) harbor misconceptions about history. This is a massive problem for teachers of social studies. How do we challenge what students think they know and believe in a way that allows them the room to grow? There are opportunities to do this through parallel sources, showing a dissonance between or among a variety of sources dealing with the same topic (Howard Zinn's *A People's History of the United States*, and the Disney televised film, on the Alamo, for example). How do we account for the differences? Where can we go to get more information to explain the differences? How do we evaluate the sources? How do we evaluate for stereotypes, bias, ideological stances, and other elements that might compromise scholarship?

The next step is to look for films that deal with topics that are related to what we want to cover and to preview them carefully. What do they say? How accurate are they? What do we as teachers need to know about the topic so that we can be comfortable ourselves with the most accurate story we can find? Are there sections of the films or documentaries that might offer something useful to our studies?

How Do You Help Students Choose
Appropriate Books for Social Studies Learning?

Tarry's response: Choosing a book to read for social studies is just like choosing a book for any other discipline. Make sure the child knows the theme and the related topics. Brainstorming with the class provides some kids with needed guidance. It often helps if the librarian or the teacher can identify books that would fit the topic, such as presidents, the Revolutionary War, or explorers. Giving book talks helps kids even more. Showing them a wide range of acceptable books and asking for their input as to why one book is "on theme" and another is not provides substantial learning. Encourage the kids to read the fly leaf, read the back of the paperback, and to thumb through the illustrations before making a choice. Also help students choose a book that they can, in fact, read in the amount of time given. Some children are slow readers, and shouldn't choose a three hundred-page book if it has to be read in a week. Teach kids how to figure out the average number of pages they'll have to read a day so they can make a logical decision. Show them how to use an index to see if the book really does tie to the theme or concept. Along with that skill, teach them the five-finger rule: Turn to any full page of text. Scan down the text, putting a finger from one hand on each word the reader doesn't know. If the reader uses all five fingers on one page, put the book away and look for a new one. The vocabulary is too tough for this kind of reading.

What About Historical Fiction in the Social Studies Classroom?

Doug's response: Many teachers use historical fiction to serve multiple duty. In some cases it presents good, solid historical information. In most cases it offers a textured, human feel for a time. The fiction offers an experience of a time or place rarely found in a textbook. We know that Lincoln was elected in 1860, but do we know anything about what it was like to walk the streets of Washington, D.C. during that election year? What would we have seen or heard on those streets? What would it have smelled like? Who would have been on the streets, and what would the streets themselves have been like? Historical fiction can help us to come closer to experiencing that walk, and that knowledge is an important part of the study of Lincoln's election.

Wonderful books have been written about key figures and times in history; many of them tell at least slightly different stories so there are questions implicit in that. How do we find the truth about things? What do these books tell us and how does that compare to our textbooks, encyclopedias, and other reference sources? How do we evaluate all the information we are receiving?

A story like *Morning Girl*, by Michael Dorris, raises this question.

177

What is accurate, historically, and what has been imagined and invented by the author? How does he know what things were like in 1492, and do all accounts agree? Do we have to have that agreement before we can teach a topic or a story? How do we help our students to deal with ambiguity, with contradiction, with the messiness of real life? We have the responsibility as teachers to become aware of the liberties taken by authors in writing their fictions, and the inaccuracies (intentional or unintentional) contained in their works so that our students are not mislead.

We also have the opportunity to help our students to learn to evaluate information and to come to understanding about what we have

FIGURE 4–2 *Leimomi Reflects on Ellis Island Exhibit*

learned. We can then model the process we go through ourselves as we struggle with the same questions. We can provide readings that present conflicting views of the same event, and have them develop strategies for resolving the conflicts, for themselves. We can teach our students to function as historians in trying to research and understand the past.

What Is Historical Literacy?

Tarry's response: It is wonderful that elementary teachers and middle-school teachers alike have found that bringing trade books into their social studies classrooms motivates and enhances student engagement. However, just because students have read a historical fiction novel does not mean they have "covered" their social studies content. Picture books are powerful, but a few picture books do not make an integrated history.

Myra Zarnowski recently stated in an article in *The New Advocate* that the challenge we face in selecting and using children's literature to teach history is to identify books that both fit our educational goals in terms of content and make the process of historical thinking visible. This means we want our kids: 1) to pay attention to sources of information; 2) recognize conflicting accounts and interpretive decisions; 3) identify powerful concepts and generalizations; and 4) discover connections between past and present.

Zarnowski recommends that teachers seek out books that present conflicting accounts so students awaken to the choices that authors make depending on their own points of view and their personal biases. She suggests that teachers not only attend to the source notes at the end of the book, but that we share these notes with our students so the kids develop an understanding of the research that underpins what they read. She advocates the use of primary documents, ones cited by the author, as a way to explore how the author used the information. Zarnowski reminds teachers to help their students discern bias, as well as slanted or emotional language. Finally, she points out that writing history is a selective process, consisting of what a writer considers significant or worth knowing. These values change over time. The social studies learner should consider the author's reasoning, time, and place to achieve a level of historical literacy.

What About Current Events?

Doug's response: Current events are certainly an important element to a classroom, but I have to say that I have some questions and concerns about them myself. I have felt sometimes that the current events were much more important to me than they were to the students and that more of the concerns addressed were adult concerns. I believe that part of our role is moving students past their limited, self-directed orbit and out into the larger world. For this reason, current events are an important part of a social studies program. However, I don't think that insisting on current events, against the clear resistance of student disinterest, is always a wise policy. As with virtually everything else, introducing and dealing with current events at a level appropriate to the students with whom you are working is a crucial element to the success of this tack. Also, some current-events issues are more important to your students than others. I am getting better at presenting issues in ways that grab my students and generate discussions. Part of this improvement is my willingness to let things go if the students are not interested, if the issue is mine alone.

Tarry's response: I agree with Doug in terms of keying in to the kids' interests. I've found that weekly news magazines like *Time for Kids* pique my students' interest. The trouble is, there is no way we have time to do *Time for Kids* every week as a current event. Sometimes we read it during reader's workshop and use it as a vehicle for learning specific reading skills. For example, I might ask my kids to highlight the three main events in the lead news article. Sometimes I hold certain issues back until we study the topic in science or social studies and read the magazine together for initial information or an extension of what we've already learned. Current events can be used effectively in the classroom as a way to give kids practice in expressing their personal convictions. Asking them to prioritize events in terms of urgency, to take a stand on a multifaceted issue, or to create a slogan to arouse public interest encourages students to think and to speak their minds. With e-mail available in many classrooms, we can encourage our kids to respond to magazine editors electronically, bringing new meaning to the *current* in current events. Perhaps more importantly, it can also teach them to listen and to respect others' opinions as well.

How Do I End a Unit of Study?

Tarry's response: In some classrooms, units end with a bang. In others, they end with a whimper or just fade away. The problem with ending is that it has a lot to do with what's been going on during the major learning of the unit. Kids need to be active during social studies. They need to be thoughtful. They need to discover new ideas and work with others. They need to see the connection between what they are learning and their own lives. In a word, kids studying social studies need to be involved!

My favorite way to end a unit includes some kind of a project, presentation, performance, or paper that lets the kids demonstrate what they know. Sometimes it's a book compiling knowledge, attitudes, and action. Sometimes it's a research report in the form of a travel brochure or an informational poster. Occasionally, we end a unit of study with a dramatic performance, poetry reading, or a story sharing when we invite in students from other classes. At other times, our unit will end with a student-written biography, a letter to the editor, or a class book. Ending a unit with a culminating activity or peak experience, something that involves using the skills and ideas learned provides students, parents, and the teacher, with a sense of closure. Do I test? Sometimes. But the test does not signal the end of the unit. The project, the presentation, performance, or paper does.

I don't think there is a one single way to end a unit, but I do believe as each unit closes the kids should have the opportunity to write a personal reflection about what he or she did, learned, and felt about that experience. Asking students to think back and write about their activities, their thinking, and their emotional response to learning helps me assess my contribution to the kids' growth, my effectiveness as a facilitator and coach, and my choices as a teacher. This information shapes our next unit as it reshapes the unit we've just finished before I teach it again. Additionally, this kind of metacognitive process creates a sense of closure for the kids as well as a recognition that they've still got more questions to investigate and additional interest and curiosity about the content. Finally, to me, a perfect ending prompts the students to action. It leads to the next step, which is independent student participation within the community, either in giving service, righting wrongs, or identifying needs.

Doug's response: I agree with Tarry's response with one caveat. I have started units of study with excellent plans and intentions only to find that they have fallen flat. I have become much more comfortable with recognizing that, for whatever reason, at this time the unit is going nowhere. I then have three options: to plow through, so that we can get to what comes next (which often depends on learning that should happen in the current unit); to rethink how to present the unit so that we still cover the content but do so in a way that is more successful; or to recognize that this is not the time for this unit of study and cut it short, without a formal ending. There is a time and place for all three responses, and it is good teaching to recognize the need to change plans when appropriate.

It is frustrating to stop short of the mark, but it can be even more frustrating (and deadly) to slog through to the end of the unit when it is clearly not working. I make what adjustments I can, but if the unit cannot be saved I will end it, as gracefully and quickly as possible so that we can move on, with the option of returning to the uncompleted unit at a later date, if appropriate.

I'm Way Behind in My Schedule. How Can I Catch Up?

Tarry's response: I assume you mean you have not covered the content your grade level is supposed to cover in a school year. If your kids have had a rich social studies experience all year, I wouldn't worry too much about being behind.

Although content is important, it's not the primary focus of elementary social studies. What we want is for our children to practice reading to learn. This includes reading related fiction and nonfiction resources, and identifying the important information. We want our kids to practice organizational skills. This includes putting information into a new format. We want our kids to practice good citizenship skills. This means they can work in a group cooperatively. This means they practice being both leaders and followers. This means they use time and materials productively, constructively, creatively. This means they will learn. They can learn content now or later. Learning how to learn, however, and loving to learn, is what I think is important. However, if you are required by your school district to complete a textbook, here's a strategy that might ease your mind:

1. Go through the chapter(s) and copy down the boldface subtitles of each section on small slips of paper. Write down the page numbers as well.

2. Put all the slips in a hat and have each kid draw one.

3. Ask the kids to turn to their page numbers and read their section, jotting down any words they don't know.

4. Go around the room asking each child to share a vocabulary word that he or she didn't know. Discuss the words.

5. Ask the kids to read their sections again. (If you have delayed readers, you may want to try buddy reading, lip reading, or reading out loud.)

6. Direct students to look at the heading or topic of their section and then restate it as a question. Share some models. Ask them to rewrite that heading as a question and check what they have written. This is where you can help those who don't quite understand.

7. Give each student a piece of the same-size notebook paper. If you want the kids to illustrate their topic, have them fold the paper in half. Immediately above the fold, have them write the question they just formed about their topic. Later, they will draw a picture on the top half and write on the lower half. Sometimes I

prefer the kids use the whole sheet of paper for writing their response.

8. Instruct the kids to answer their questions, summarizing the information. I have my kids do this in pencil and in cursive. Of course, word processing is an alternative. It depends on my objectives.

9. As students finish, they reread their composition, revising as needed. Then the students bring their piece to me and we edit together.

10. After editing, the kids go over their pencil-written copy in fine-tip black felt pen. This way they don't make new mistakes.

11. On the top half of the paper, they draw a picture to help readers understand the topic. This drawing needs to be in black felt tip so it copies well.

12. When the class has completed the assignment, I photocopy their pages back-to-back in chronological order, making a text for each student.

This student-created book is what my kids study, not our formal textbook. Instead of being 120 pages long, it's fifteen pages or so. The kids love the idea of writing their own text. It validates their writing, their thinking, and their ability to teach each other. And it's one way to "finish the text."

How Do I Teach Point of View?

Doug's response: Social studies must communicate clearly that point of view is an essential element of any story. Who is telling the story (about Columbus, Bunker Hill, Hiroshima, smart bombs, the Bay of Pigs, the three little pigs) and their relationship to that story is important. Whose voices we are *not* hearing are as important as the voices we hear most often.

Students can practice point of view quite effectively and practice language-arts skills at the same time. Consider assigning the kids the task of writing a letter as if they were Pocahontas or John Smith. Try having them keep a journal as they read a historical fiction novel, as

FIGURE 4–3 *LaToya Finishing a Collage*

if they were the main character, or another character in the story. Publish point-of-view newspapers. For example, after studying the Civil War, have the kids create three different front pages of a newspaper: one from the northern point of view, one from the southern, and one from a free-black point of view.

How Often Do I Have to Teach Social Studies?

Tarry's response: Most states actually have guidelines that require a minimum amount of time devoted to each discipline. Check with your principal. However, note that these are usually minimum amounts of time. If social studies becomes the center of your day, then you will find you are teaching social studies all day long. Actually, if you think about ordinary things you do in your classroom, like deciding how the kids should pass in their papers, line up for lunch, participate in class decisions, or organize a food drive, you'll discover you are doing social studies all day long. Social studies, from our perspective, is more than content. It's also how we treat each other, how we make decisions, and what happens when we're doing something else. (Or as I once heard, social studies is what we do when no one else is looking.)

In my classroom, social studies permeates everything we do. When my students are practicing writing traits, they are usually writing on a social studies topic. When my students read, they are usually doing research on a social studies topic or reading a related novel. When my students make a formal presentation, it is usually centered on social studies issues. Even when we do science, I bring in a social studies piece: the civics of that science topic as we explore the related issues around what we are studying. For example, we raise and release salmon in our classroom as part of a unit having to do with watersheds, the environment, and the science of salmon. We also investigate the civics of salmon, identifying the people, and their agendas, who are most concerned about the plight of the salmon.

Doug's response: Social studies can be the hub of your entire school day, with every topic organized around a central theme or concept. There is nothing that is not social studies. Everything happens in context, in an interdependent and interrelated world.

When you are reading a book, help the students to understand the relationships and dynamics of the people involved. This is social studies. Frequently there are class or race or gender issues, also the stuff of social studies. What is the town like where the story takes place? What kinds of work do the people do in this story? Is Mom home cooking dinner and sewing Halloween costumes? Is she working as a cleaning woman for the rich folks across town? Is she the chief financial officer of a computer software company? All these are social studies issues. If the story is taking place in a location very different than the one in which the story is being read, how do we understand those differences? What would the story be like if it were taking place in your town? How might the story be changed?

Talk with the students about the research the author had to do to write the story. What did he or she need to know about the people, about the place, about the issues covered in the story? How does one do that kind of research? What kinds of stories might the students write, and where would they go about doing the kinds of research needed to carry out the project?

I helped a third-grade teacher who was working with her students on researching various animals. She had them write stories starring their animals, and had to include aspects of their previous research. The story could not contradict the research (though of course it was okay for the animals to talk). They had to make sure the setting was accurate for their animals (no whales in the desert), their diet was correct, and that at least some of the other animals in the story belonged there. The students were third graders and there was a great deal of poetic license taken, but the research served as the backbone of many of the stories. It was a nice blending of social studies, science, and language arts.

I Seem to Run out of Time for Social Studies. What Should I Do?

Tarry's response: It sounds like social studies is an isolated subject in your classroom. Consider mixing social studies and reading together. For example, if you have a basal or class reader, go through the reader and identify stories that somehow connect to topics you teach in social studies. Instead of reading your basal, one story after another, skip around so that your reading connects with your social studies. If you don't have a basal, choose chapter books that connect. If that doesn't work for you, try reading related books aloud to your kids. These can be fiction or nonfiction.

I have found that it is practically impossible for me to keep a science unit and a social studies unit going at the same time. Because I know that active, meaningful, and challenging activities are crucial to student interest and student learning, I just can't keep the focus. So I don't. I teach social studies for two to four weeks and then I do a science unit. I tell my parents at curriculum night what I am doing and why. So far, I've had no complaints and the kids love it! We can keep major projects in progress all day, not having to clean off our desks and switch midstream to another discipline.

Another possibility is to start your day with social studies. Think about it. Maybe it will be current events. For example, have the kids read their weekly newsmagazine when they come in (*Time for Kids*, *Scholastic News*). Then choose one of the topics for a class debate. I have my kids choose where they stand, pro or con, or somewhere in between. And stand they do, along an imaginary continuum. Then they take turns speaking, sharing why they have chosen the position they have. By alternating the reasons between the pros and the cons, a balanced presentation is provided. My students have an opportunity to express their opinions in a public forum. There is no right or wrong answer. They practice democratic citizenship as they learn to think on their feet.

My Kids Don't Like Social Studies.

Doug's response: It may be more accurate to say that they have not liked their past experiences with social studies. Find out what they are interested in and make it the center of a complex, integrated unit that allows them to investigate that which interests them, be it blues music, baseball, the history of Barbie, basketball, painting, or construction. Allow them to learn about the world through their interests and passions, whenever possible. There are no topics that exist in isolation, and the trick of social studies is to connect everything. Using a thematic, integrative approach allows one to study anything starting anywhere.

I worked with older students to investigate products such as the coffee they drink, the Barbie dolls they played with as young children, and the clothes they were currently wearing. The students researched the history of the clothing, learned the realities of production, looking at question such as these:

Who makes Barbie dolls?

Where are they made?

How are they made?

What are the lives like for the people who make the dolls?

What were their lives like before Barbie?

Why are the dolls made where they are (entirely outside of the United States)?

How does Barbie get to the stores in your town?

Why are they priced as they are?

Who makes the profit?

The students then presented their findings to their classmates in a nonwritten format, using visual storyboards, plays, slide shows, art constructions, and music.

The level of the activity should be adjusted to fit the abilities of the students. A major research project may be inappropriate for third graders, but there are aspects of their world they can research, at least a little.

How Can I Teach Reading During Social Studies?

Tarry's response: Students who can read and comprehend their reading are more successful social studies learners. One major way we can make social studies learning more fun, more effective, and more efficient is to use groups as integral to the reading process. This means decreasing the number of times we do round-robin oral reading of the textbook in class. This means increasing the number of times we set up partner or buddy reading. My daughter who teaches third grade uses round-the-clock reading buddies. Each student gets a blank clock-face ditto sheet. They are given time to go around the room and find a buddy for each of the twelve hours on the clock. Both buddies need to agree on the hour and write each other's name down on that hour for future reference. When it's time for paired reading, Tani simply chooses an "hour" and the kids buddy up. "Today the three o'clock people will read together. You may take turns reading to each other or you may read out loud together, but you must read the handout and then write down three things you learned."

How About an Example of
Teaching Social Studies During Reading?

Tarry's response: One strategy I like to use is having the kids read silently but pairing them up for discussion and agreement on the main idea of each segment, chapter, or section of the resource we're using. I pair my students by reading speed. I ask the kids to read the first section and I watch to see who finishes first, second, and so on. I jot down pairs of children who finish at about the same time. I have found that a sure recipe for disaster is to pair my fastest reader with a slow reader. Someone is sure to get into trouble. But if two kids read at relatively the same rate, then the pressure is off. They can read and

FIGURE 4–4 *Finishing Touches*

190

discuss at their own, comfortable pace. I can monitor their progress easily by having them write down the main idea or event for each segment. A child who needs more time can read at home or during a study time, and discuss his or her ideas the next day with a buddy. That way, individual differences are honored as the work of the class moves on. Best of all, two objectives are being accomplished simultaneously. One, the kids are reading a book related to our social studies content, learning more about the topic. Two, the kids are helping each other achieve greater comprehension of what they've read than either would have alone.

Can You Tell Me More About Reading and Social Studies?

Tarry's response: Reading is an essential, integral part of any social studies curriculum. Whether being read to, reading alone, or reading with others, social studies students utilize the written word to acquire and use information. The textbook is certainly one source, but we use many others as well.

Picture books make sense at the primary level, but many teachers of intermediate and middle-school kids wonder how these books can help them teach social studies at the center. One of the paramount skills in social studies is the ability to acquire information. Specific reading skills related to comprehension and vocabulary are critical. Picture books are great for introducing a concept and extending it beyond the textbook. Picture books flesh out history, illuminate geography, amplify cultures, and point out political issues. Whether the teacher reads a picture book aloud, students share books, or they read alone, picture books begin the process of involving students in the social studies curriculum. They also stimulate critical thinking as the class evaluates the information in picture books and decides how to decide whether the information is reliable.

Most textbooks represent only one point of view. It's up to teachers to introduce other viewpoints and reading is one way to do that. Reading historical novels or first-person accounts of historical events provides glimpses into other points of view. Reading these kinds of resources aloud makes it possible to impart information that may be too difficult for some kids to read alone. Reading aloud also invites frequent conversation breaks during which the teacher stops and checks for comprehension, inviting the listeners to respond from their own experiences. Reading aloud also encourages teachers to "talk the walk" by thinking out loud as new vocabulary is encountered, main ideas are found, and details in sequence are identified, so kids learn how to learn from reading.

Biographies add to the richness of the social studies curriculum. Most social studies texts do not contain biographies. At best they can devote one page to a person who exemplifies some admirable quality or who lived during an eventful time. Trade book biographies found in the school library, on the other hand, are often short (usually sixty-four pages in the standard format), fairly easy to read (about fourth-grade level), and contain some photographs to help students form a graphic time line. New, picture book-format biographies are becoming increasingly available. These, however, are often more challenging to read. Frequently, they include more "gossipy" information. Teachers have a wide array of choices when using biographies in the classroom. Sometimes, teachers have the students read on a theme, like powered flight. Sometimes there is a collection of different books about a single person, such as Abraham Lincoln. At other times, biographies may focus on an event, such as the writing of the Constitution.

My Kids Can't Read the Text. What Do I Do?

Doug's response: If you focus on helping them to read what they *can* read, at whatever level, about topics of interest to them, they will be more likely to read successfully. Students can pick topics that matter to them, find books or articles about those topics, and read, with or without help. You can also have them write about these topics, either on their own or through dictation, and that can become subsequent reading assignments. They can work with others on projects, and one of the aspects of the assignments can focus on their partners helping them to read material.

This is a difficult issue that has many facets. One of the issues may center on what you are presenting to your students to read; the social studies text may prove more (or less) than they can handle. Historical fiction, biographies, or other books or materials may be more involving, covering the same time period or topic in ways that invite students to read more.

It is also possible that there are things that you can do as a teacher to support their efforts as readers. Perhaps more to the point is that one of the major tasks of elementary teachers is to teach reading, and there is every reason to use social studies content (trade books, stories, student writing) as the reading material. The challenge is to find interesting materials that engage the students and encourage them to read, and to have that material be readable. When in doubt, I read to my kids. I read picture books, novels, and even the text, at times.

What Do You Think of Departmentalization?

Tarry's response: It really depends on your situation. If you decide to departmentalize I'd urge you to combine social studies and language-arts period into a block, extending the time beyond one period. If possible, I'd throw in reading class as well. I don't see how anyone can teach social studies without teaching language arts . . . or reading. Social studies content gives a reason to write, a focus for reading.

I also have concerns about programs that put students into social studies classes for forty-five minutes a day. That time constraint does not allow for hands-on, active social studies. Kids need to "get into" social studies. They need time in class to make three-dimensional maps out of salt dough, create puppets for plays they've written about problems regarding the Constitution, and construct posters revealing what they know about the Iroquois Confederation. They need to work together, solving problems and sharing information as they go. Each of those activities takes more than forty-five minutes.

How Can I Teach Ancient
History to Modern Children?

Doug's response: This is one of the most frequently asked questions. I don't have a good answer to the larger question, which is, "Why teach what you care little about and about which the kids care little?" One good step is to find ways in which you are interested in the social studies you are expected to teach. What aspects of ancient civilizations catch your curiosity or interest? It might be government, agriculture, religion, art, music, architecture, the ways in which women or children were treated, or anything else. Begin with your own interests, and enter into a study of that aspect of that time and place. You will be a more effective teacher if you are teaching something that matters to you.

Thematic teaching raises more fundamental questions about why societies develop the way they do, and in this way the topic can be turned modern (and perhaps of more interest to you and to the children). How do we meet our various societal and individual needs, and how did those ways evolve or develop? How did this happen at various points around the world? What kind of ideal society is possible? What do all societies have in common?

Tarry's response: Teachers can turn kids on to any subject by their own enthusiasm, energy, and information. Entice the kids through an engaging hook to consider the topic. Open the topic for personal exploration. Encourage the kids to construct their own meaning. Move beyond the textbook to multiple ways of knowing. Engage in hands-on learning. Structure small group cooperation. Integrate the learning with other disciplines throughout the day. Provide time for reflection. Use these classroom structures and your kids will love ancient history, or anything else you study.

How Does Research Fit In?

Doug's response: It begins with students learning to identify useful and interesting questions, develop and carry out research strategies that allow for gathering the most complete body of information, and to research without prejudgment. The first step involves choosing a topic and developing a beginning set of questions. Then the questioner formulates a research plan based on a task analysis (what do I know, how do I know it, who might have some knowledge, who can help me to find out more, where can I look). Students must learn to enter this process prepared to evaluate what they have asked and what they are finding; then editing and changing their initial plan if it is not serving them well. Open-ended research can lead to unanticipated interests or information that changes the question or focus of the search in midstream. Finally, students must come to know when they have done enough, when it is time to gather together what they have found, to edit it to its essential elements, and to communicate it in a form that is most effective and powerful.

Open-ended research means that you are not looking for what you already know. The students have to be given the opportunity to learn the skills, methods, and challenges of research. There is a wide range of assignments requiring varying degrees of research, and these can be introduced throughout the beginning of the year. Students love to learn more about those things they care most about, and I try to take advantage of their interests whenever possible when the objective is to introduce a research technique or resource. I also try to have the assignment create a need to know for the students, so that they want to carry out the research.

Research assignments that are mostly fact based have their place, but rarely inspire a need to know.

How Do I Help My Kids Do Successful Research?

Tarry's response: I find with beginning researchers, like my fifth graders, it works well if we identify the key points that we are going to research. To accomplish this, we might start with a mind map (a graphic organizer that requires students to brainstorm about a topic or concept and to classify their ideas into clusters), a KWL chart, or first-thoughts writing (prior knowledge is revealed as the students jot down quickly the first thoughts they have when asked to consider a topic or concept), and brainstorm questions with a partner or two. From these compilations, we often develop a list of topics or questions to answer. Research starts, using books, encyclopedias, electronic media, and sometimes interviews. I don't let my students copy full sentences from any source. Data collection, bits of information, and facts are stressed. I frequently give the kids data sheets with limited amounts of space to write to in, discouraging copying out of the book. Also, I don't let the kids begin writing up their research until all notes have been taken and the references put away. (My kids do all their writing in our classroom. I want to observe their style, prompt them when they have problems, and celebrate their moments of brilliance.)

I've found giving kids choices for their research topics very motivational. Even if the kids have no idea, say, of who any explorers are besides Columbus, giving them a choice infuses the assignment with more enthusiasm. I frequently show choices on the overhead projector: countries in Asia, states in the union, explorers, aspects of colonial life, presidents, and so forth. Turning the overhead on, I draw kids' names out of our "lottery box." The child chosen picks the topic he or she wants to investigate. I always try to have more choices than kids. That way the child who is chosen last still has a choice.

Help! I Have to Cover Too Much in One Year. What Should I Do?

Tarry's response: I have a series of suggestions that fall along a continuum. One long-term solution is to get on the district social studies curriculum committee and change the breadth of the expectations. These committees often have few elementary teachers sitting on them. It's been my experience that elementary input is valued. A more immediate idea is to meet with others at your grade level and determine what the most significant events, people, and core knowledge are within each concept. This collaboration will provide consensus on what the teachers at your school think is important to teach and what can be left out. Recently, educators have concluded that the survey course isn't the best practice. Instead, a technique called "postholes in history" is recommended. Instead of having students memorize an unconnected number of factoids, select a major issue or turning point upon which your kids can construct their own understanding of U.S. history. Choose a limited number of these to teach in your classroom. Or select a theme, like exploration, inventions, or colonial life.

What Does Your Daily Schedule Look Like?

Tarry's response: I teach in a self-contained classroom, so I have much more freedom than lots of teachers. I work hard to protect at least one hour a day where I have all my kids. That time is when we have what I call Flow. This is my name for the time I can carve out of our daily schedule so my kids can get into the flow of learning a specific theme or concept. For me, Flow is a combination of social studies and/or science, art, and language arts. Recognizing that it doesn't happen exactly the same time every day, here's what my daily schedule might look like:

9:20 to 10:20	Math
10:20 to 10:55	Specialist
10:55 to 11:10	Recess
11:10 to 11:30	SSR
11:30 to 12:45	Flow
12:45 to 1:30	Lunch and Recess
1:30 to 2:30	Reader's Workshop
2:30 to 2:45	Recess
2:45 to 3:30	Spelling/Handwriting

You'll notice that I don't have a specific language arts period. I truly do teach all my language arts through the content areas. My reading, while a separate period, is tied to whatever we are studying during Flow time, so that many times the reader's workshop is an extension of Flow.

How Do You Manage Cooperative Groups, Especially During Projects?

Tarry's response: Most often, projects require small cooperative-group work. I determine what the goals are for each day, or I ask the students to tell me what their daily goals are. I can set deadlines for each part of the project or I can require my student groups to agree on deadlines. I can decide what the final product will be, or I can encourage my student groups to fashion their own product based on criteria I have selected or my class has agreed upon. In this criteria, I always include one or two behaviors, such as uses time well in class; helps group solve problems; contributes positively to the group goal. I often keep a criteria sheet on each group and either fill it out from my observations, ask a group member to fill it out based on his or her observations, or ask each member of the group to fill one out at the end of work period. (I wish I could do this record keeping daily, but I just don't seem to be able to get it together. I'm finding the kids are much more reliable about recording than I am.)

It is not unusual for me to call a group together, especially one that seems fragmented and unproductive, for a conference based on these observations to determine what needs to happen to help the group be more successful. Groups that are democratic, productive, and fun are critical to the essence of social studies education: the practice of participatory citizenship.

What Are Some Alternatives to the Lecture Format?

Tarry's response: Most teachers of K–8 children know that lecturing simply doesn't work very effectively, even if it is efficient. If the lecture were less than ten minutes, children could probably tolerate it. Unfortunately, most of us get on a roll and can't stop at ten minutes. Hence, the birth of the minilesson. Often employed as one part of a discipline-based workshop (reader's workshop, writer's workshop, history workshop), the minilesson is a presentation by the teacher (or a guest or a student) introducing a specific skill, sharing a body of knowledge, or demonstrating a product. *Mini* is the operative prefix here: no more than ten minutes. Then the kids move on to their own investigations, applying the recently shared information where and when appropriate.

Do I Have to Use Cooperative Groups All the Time?

Tarry's response: Although cooperative groups are desirable, they don't have to be used all the time. I think that individual inquiry is equally important. However, individual inquiry may feed into the group, rather than be a direct exchange with the teacher. Independent, individual investigations should be interwoven with group work to provide a well-balanced educational experience for our students.

My Students All Choose the Same Group. How Do You Handle This?

Tarry's response: Sometimes I limit the size of a group before we begin choosing. Sometimes I use gentle persuasion: "Oh my, one of the most interesting questions hasn't been selected by anyone. This is a really fun one. I wonder if anyone would be willing to try it?" Occasionally, I set up arbitrary membership: "Groups must have at least two boys and two girls." Or must have one person who likes to draw, one who likes to write, one who knows how to cut and paste on the computer, and one who is willing to read aloud to the group. Sometimes I just throw the topic out if no one wants it. If it's crucial to the study we're doing, I'll find another strategy and another time to bring it in.

My Kids Argue and Don't Get Anything Accomplished. Do Yours?

Tarry's response: Sure, they do. These arguments tend to fall into one of two categories: content oriented or more personal. The personal category usually has to do with working in groups, reaching common goals, contributing to the success of a project, taking on leadership roles or participant roles. I think that we as teachers have a real obligation to help our students learn to work in groups. By the time kids are intermediate and middle-school age, we can be pretty direct in our feedback to our kids: "Hiram, I notice that you are often goofing off when the rest of your group is working. What can you do to change your participation and make it more productive?" "Sally, it seems like I hear you arguing with members of your group frequently. Can you tell me what's going on?"

Content arguments are wonderful. As long as they don't deteriorate into personal "tirades," content arguments should be encouraged. Hearing the kids debate within their small groups or getting passionate about their opinions is what social studies is all about. Helping them keep cool while arguing and teaching them how to present their point of view effectively is also what social studies is all about. Practice is ongoing in most classrooms. Content arguments also reveal the level of comprehension students have acquired. Misinformation, misused vocabulary, or erroneous conclusions point to a need for revisiting segments of the unit.

What Are the "Big Questions" in Social Studies?

Tarry's response: Content-oriented problem solving has to do with "big questions." Big questions are often evaluative in nature: Did the Civil War deeply hurt or help the United States? Did Columbus have an obligation to the native peoples he met when he came ashore? Big questions frequently are stated as suppositions: If you had been Pocahantas, would you have gone to England? Why or why not? If you had been a northeastern woodland Native American, would you have fought for England or the colonists? Give reasons. Big questions often ask students to reveal different points of view about history or culture. Write two letters: one as if you were a Taino Indian and had just witnessed Columbus coming ashore, the other as if you were the cabin boy on Columbus' ship and you had just come ashore. Compare and contrast the Cherokee way of life with that of the white settlers. Do you think conflict was inevitable? Big questions often have no right answer. These are the kinds of questions that require students to draw upon a reservoir of knowledge, marshall ideas and arguments, and think critically. These are the kinds of questions that reveal the depth of knowledge students have and their ability to use that knowledge. These are the kinds of questions our students meet in expository exams. We need to give students an opportunity to show what they know. Whether they are writing independently, creating a skit in a small group, or participating in a mock Senate hearing, it's important there be some opportunity for students to demonstrate their growth intellectually and personally. This is assessment that is authentic, challenging, and meaningful.

I'm Overwhelmed. How Do I Deal With All of This?

Doug's response: One of the most basic steps a teacher can take when dealing with all of this is to look for ways to serve many needs with one activity, or one unified course of study. When we study space, immigration, homelessness, colonialism, world geography, or other units, we are carrying out our spelling, language-arts, science, social studies, art, and math lessons. When the lessons are integrated, centered on the same topic, I suddenly have more time.

An extended project, made up of many smaller steps, means there is a more comprehensive and efficient planning process, making it more possible to stay focused. I feel pulled in fewer directions.

What Are Democratic Values and What Does It Mean to Teach Them?

Doug's response: One should not lecture about learning styles, nor dictate about living in a democratic manner. If we want students to learn about being citizens in a democracy, we must give them real opportunities to practice, to make decisions, to learn and exercise critical thinking. Students must have the opportunity to deal with the consequences of their choices and the complexities of being an individual within a group that is within an institution.

We shy away from practicing democratic values in the classroom because it can be messy, and students may make choices we don't like. There are clear power issues involved in this discussion. We are the teachers and adults in the classroom, and we are hired to teach; our classrooms can never be complete democracies because of this essential power imbalance. Students can still have many opportunities to make meaningful decisions about what they study, how their classroom operates, and how they can work together most effectively. The teacher must be clear about those decisions he or she is responsible for without input. The teacher is then able to open up the decision-making process on other decisions. These decisions (to be made by the group) should include decisions of real substance

FIGURE 4–5 *Xavier Maps the Room*

and meaning for the students. A list of possible student decisions could include:

deciding what jobs are needed in the classroom and how they will be filled

topics for study (from a list generated initially by the teacher)

times for certain activities

problem-solving policies and approaches

social action agendas and strategies, and class rules and discipline policy (again recognizing that the teacher will have certain non-negotiables in this area)

How Can I Learn More About Teaching Social Studies?

Tarry's response: First, take advantage of the classes and workshops offered in your area to learn more. Many times, the social studies-related in-service programs are free or very reasonably priced. Local professional associations, like the state or regional Council for the Social Studies are good sources of information. Frequently they publish newsletters with helpful resources identified. Read other professional journals. In the next chapter, see a list of professional organizations that provide teachers with support. Many of these feature summer learning opportunities in their winter and spring issues. Want to go to Japan for free? Want to study at Valley Forge or Monticello? Interested in attending law school for teachers? There are myriad opportunities for those who are willing to take a chance.

Second, talk to the teachers down the hall. Find out what they do. Often there are one or two teachers on a staff who make social studies come alive for their students. Spend some time with them. Walk by their classrooms frequently and see what they have displayed on their walls and bulletin boards. More than likely, they'll be pleased to share their experience and materials. Join listserves on the Internet. Work to develop a collegial relationship with those teachers at your grade level. Two heads really are better than one! And two or three people, working together to fashion a unit, often succeed beyond any individual dream.

Third, think about your social studies while driving to work or taking a shower. Play with ideas. You might want to get an overview first by reading the table of contents of your social studies text and scanning the chapter overviews. Then look for related resources. If it's history, look for time lines. If it's geography, grab an atlas. Go to your school library and look at the appropriate Dewey decimal sections. Ask the librarian to pull books for you to peruse. Children's books are a wonderful, quick way to get an idea of what may be important. If all else fails, open the trusty encyclopedia (either print or electronic). Dip into the Internet if you have it available.

What About Time Scheduled for Specialists?

Tarry's response: Don't worry about what you can't control. Capitalize on what connections you can create. Doug and I think it's best to start small. Trying to integrate the whole day all at once is a sure recipe for frustration and failure. Start by looking at reading or writing and figure out where you can slip one or two of those skills you have to do anyway in with some social studies content. Look at the strategies in the next chapter. You might find an idea that works for you. It'll come. Just give yourself time and keep open to opportunities for integration. Good luck!

Chapter Bibliography

ZARNOWSKI, MYRA. 1998. "Coming out from Under the Spell of Stories." *The New Advocate*. Fall: 345–57.

FIVE

Our Favorite Strategies, Resources, and Websites

Postscript: Dear Reader,

Once again we present you with a chapter that is not a traditional chapter. This time we are displaying for your enjoyment and edification an annotated compilation of sixty-eight practical teaching strategies that engage our kids while we put social studies at the center. Use them, change them, make them your own. Just remember, kids' brains love novelty, they like doing things differently. On the other hand, we need to use every moment we have with them productively. These strategies fill both needs.

We also share with you some of the most helpful professional books we've read, ones that have touched our lives, both in and out of school. Finally, we wanted to give you the addresses to our essential websites, places, and people who enrich our own understanding of the world in which we live.

Enjoy!

T.L.L. and D.S.

Strategies That Put Social Studies at the Center

Personalizing Events

Ask your students to write about a historical event through the eyes of a citizen who is there: at a slave auction, at Gettysburg, on the Trail of Tears, at Fort Sumter, in the Dust Bowl, waiting for the signal to begin the Oklahoma land rush. Ask them to discuss how they are feeling as well as the whats and the whys. This kind of activity helps young writers develop voice as well as becoming aware of word choice.

Conflict Resolution

Practice role-plays in the classroom modeling peaceful ways to solve problems. Use classroom and playground problems. We use an acronym, S.T.A.K.E., in our classroom:

Stop, take time to solve a problem;

Talk softly;

Ask key questions;

Keep an open mind;

Evaluate options and choose a solution all agree to live with.

Caring for Others

Set up buddies with a younger class or have kids adopt a class for which they do nice things. We read with our buddies, help with art projects, write with them, and go on short nature walks. Often times, these pals remain special friends throughout their remaining school years.

Surveys

These are a wonderful way to integrate math, language arts, and social studies. Kids each choose an issue of interest: third graders choose Beanie Babies, fifth graders choose a favorite radio station, sixth graders research information about the Holocaust. Students develop a hypothesis, generate a survey, distribute the survey to a reliable sample, evaluate the results, and write a scientific abstract regarding the process. For help, contact John Swang at his e-mail address, nsrcmms@aol.com, or website, http://youth.net/nsrc/nsrc.html. His fax number is 504-898-6420 and phone is 504-898-6437. He has created the National Student Research Center, which combines pure science, either survey or experimental design, and writing for a purpose. He's very willing to share templates, samples, and support.

Paper Dolls

Creating paper dolls as historical characters is very engaging. Whether studying the colonial period or ancient Greeks, asking kids to create a character dressed appropriately for the times ignites all kinds of writing activities, experiences with point of view, and appreciation of culture.

Phony Phone Conversations

A quick way to check reading comprehension is to ask two students to pretend they are two characters in the book you are reading. Using discarded telephones or telephone receivers, have the kids discuss another character or event in the book.

Interior Monologues

The more mature students will enjoy this activity. Ask the students if they ever have conversations inside their heads, if they ever think both sides of a conversation. Mention that many of us do, and it is often very helpful. We can plan, ramble on, or revise without anyone ever knowing but us! This process is called interior monologue. There are two formats:

1. One character or writer pretends that he or she is talking to someone else. The narrator introduces himself or herself and then proceeds to tell the other person some of his or her innermost thoughts.
2. The student actually writes his or her own thoughts about the topic or the issue. Students do not need to introduce themselves, they are simply talking inside their own minds. It is the depth of thought that matters. I encourage my kids to do stream-of-consciousness–style writing, ignoring conventions and using ellipses or dashes.

After-Dinner Conversations

Older kids like this one. Assign or have the kids choose a character from a novel or a person from history. Pretend several of them have just finished a wonderful dinner and now they are sitting around the table, talking. Eavesdrop on their conversation. Teachers may want to give some topics or questions to discuss. We thank Oralee Kramer and Rick Moulden for sharing this strategy.

One-Page Plays

Writing one-page plays is productive, especially with issues as topics. I have my kids create three characters. They must identify a problem and solve it, and they must do it on one piece of paper (one side if word processed, two if handwritten). When the kids turn in their pages, make three copies of each play. Distribute the parts to other kids and have them practice oral reading. These plays make great puppet plays or readers theater.

Puppet Plays

Puppet plays provide students with an opportunity to practice oral reading as well as work in cooperative groups. If the kids are creating their own script, then understanding how stories work, developing characters, structuring plot, writing dialogue, and a host of conventional language-arts skills are needed. When the play focuses on a social studies theme or concept, the kids demonstrate their understanding of what is being studied.

I like Chinese shadow puppets. Using an old white sheet suspended from the metal supports that holds up the acoustical tiles on my classroom ceiling for a screen and my overhead for a light source, my kids cut puppets from old manila folders. It's a charming strategy that introduces the kids to a cultural art form. Two helpful resources are produced by National School Products (800-627-9393) *China: Home of the Dragon*, a CD-ROM with brilliant images and sounds of royalty-free pictures suitable for desktop publishing, slide shows, and so forth at $29, and *Chinese Shadow Puppet Theater* ($24.95), through which you and your class can visit Asia's puppet theaters, enjoy an animated play, design puppets, and print out templates.

Story Ladders and Storyboards

Analyzing or taking a story apart is an appropriate activity for middle-grade and middle-school youngsters. The storyboard can be an eight-panel analysis with the following panel designations:

1. title and author
2. main character
3. setting
4. situation
5. problem
6. conflict
7. resolution
8. reader's critique

Using words and pictures, or pictures only, students can demonstrate their comprehension of the picture book or novel. Story ladders are a simplification of the storyboard, consisting of four panels. I ask my students to show the four most important parts of the story using pictures and words.

Diaries

Another good comprehension-checking strategy is asking the kids to write a journal or diary as if they were the main character. I like to cut regular notebook paper in half and cover it with tagboard to simulate a real journal. Using a paper punch, I make a couple of holes and fasten the whole booklet with brads. This way we can add more paper when needed. Creating a hinge by cutting one inch off the cover and then reattaching it with a piece of masking tape makes the booklet easy to open and read. My kids write in their journals or diaries in first person, as if they were the main character. They try to hit three topics: what the main character did in the chapter, what the main character knew or learned, and how the main character felt. Trading or sharing journal entries each day guarantees that most of your readers will be "on board."

ABC Charts

ABC charts or books are an engaging way to check for understanding. Used as either a vocabulary "catcher" or as a cumulative piece, the ABCs demonstrate a student's ability to organize and present information about a specific topic. I have my kids fold a piece of 18" × 24" paper into thirty-two sections. Twenty-six of those sections each represent a letter of the alphabet. The remaining sections become the title and author piece. Examples of my students' ABCs include the ABCs of Native Americans (a collection and comparison of regional Native American cultural traits, arts, and crafts), ABCs of the Human Body, ABCs of Internment, ABCs of the Northwest Forest.

Quick-and-Quiet Books

Sometimes the textbook is all we have to work with, often due to time constraints. One way to personalize the information so students find it more engaging as well as giving them practice in summarizing is the quick-and-quiet book. Go through the text and copy each major heading on a piece of paper. Write the page number down. Keep going until you have a heading for every kid in your class. Put the slips of paper into a hat and have a drawing. Tell the kids to read the section that's listed, rewrite the heading as a question, and then answer the question on a half-sheet of notebook paper. I have my kids fold a piece of notebook paper in half and write on the bottom half of the paper. Above the fold they write their newly stated question, their name as author, and draw a picture or symbol of their topic. By having the kids write their first draft in pencil, I can free them up for a "shoulder" edit (they stand by me and read their draft aloud and we correct any errors together). Then they can go over what they wrote in fine-tip black felt pen or can word process their work. I put all of the students' finished drafts into a booklet so they can study it rather than the textbook. The kids love it. They've written their own textbook!

Pop-Ups

Pop-ups are an engaging and effective way to have students become involved in a topic. Whether doing pop-ups of geographic land forms, regions of the United States, animals in their natural habitats, problems immigrants face, or the most important part from a chapter in a book, pop-ups use the kinesthetic energy that is present in every classroom. Use Joan Irvine's paperback, *How to Make*

Pop-Ups (1987) and you'll be ready to introduce this strategy to your class tomorrow.

Postcards, Baseball Cards, and Bookmarks

Postcards, baseball cards, and bookmarks are all quick strategies to check for comprehension. As kids finish their reading, ask them to make a postcard, a baseball card, or a bookmark showing one thing they learned or one question they have from their reading. I keep precut paper in my classroom (leftovers from other projects) for this purpose. This strategy also helps keep those faster readers involved while the slower ones have a chance to finish without feeling so rushed.

Quartiles

Take an ordinary piece of notebook paper. Fold it in half horizontally. Then fold that piece in half and you have a quartile, a four-page booklet. I use this minibook for checking understanding and for student reflections. Instead of having the kids ask, "Do we have to?" after instructing them to take out a piece of notebook paper and write a three-paragraph reflection on a recent project, I just have them fold a quartile and ask them to write their name and a topic heading on the first page, write what they did on the second page, what they learned on the third page, and how they feel on the last page. *Voila!* We have three painless paragraphs.

Informational Picketing

Bring activism to your classroom through informational picketing. We have used this strategy to bring environmental concerns to our communities' consciousness and health practices to our students' awareness. After studying the causes and possible solutions of a community, regional, national, or global issue, use tagboard for the kids to each make two placards exhorting people to desirable behaviors ("Give a hoot, don't pollute!" "Cigarettes kill!"). We bring in an advertising artist to show our kids the elements of effective design. After each kid has created two placards, we staple them to lightweight wooden stakes. Then we target a time and place: Earth Day, a walk from our school to the community recycling center, or the Great American Smoke Out, picketing where buses and parents drop kids at school. (Be sure to get permission to do this and discuss appropriate behavior before the event.)

Interviews, Mock Interviews

Interviews are a wonderful way to involve kids in hands-on research. Try doing model interviews in class so the kids get the idea. Brainstorm a series of questions so that the kids can select a few for their interview. Be sure to include safety tips: Don't allow students to go to an interview unaccompanied by an adult. Mock interviews are also fun and productive. I like my kids to do mock interviews after reading biographies. Just like real interviews, we brainstorm a list of questions and the kids pick six they want to ask the main character. Then

FIGURE 5–1 *Andie Works on a World Problem Poster*

they answer the questions as if they were the main character. It's great writing practice.

Storytelling

Storytelling is an art as well as a skill. Different from reading a book, storytelling connects kids to content in a special way. I always start storytelling from the heart and from the home. My kids tell family stories. Frequently they draw picture storyboards to help them remember the important parts. Work on eye contact, changes in voice, pacing, and volume (preferably, not all at once). Invite a storyteller into class. Many cities and towns have storyteller leagues who will provide people to the classroom for little or no money. One form of Japanese storytelling is done with storycards. Called *kamishibai* (ka-me-she-by), it is a delightful form of an ancient art. A resource for authentic kamishibai in English and in Japanese is Kamishibai for Kids, PO Box 20069, Park West Station, New York, NY 10025-1510. Telephone and Fax: 212-662-5836. The cards run about $35 per set.

Mock Senate Hearings

Bring real issues into the classroom by staging mock senate debates. Select three to four volunteers to be senators, representing different states. The rest of the class breaks into special interest groups. For example, when examining the spotted owl issue the class represented loggers, managed forest owners, environmentalists, and ski lodge operators. The "senators" hear the diverse and persuasive points of view, deliberate, and make a decision, which they explain to all participants.

Mock Trials

While mock trials are very popular with kids, I use them very sparingly in my classroom. Their adversarial nature tends to polarize a class and that's not what I am working for in my room. I am working for harmony, cooperation, and generosity of spirit. Mock trials tend to foster competition. However, the mock trial does provide for high-level critical and creative thinking and allows for important issues to enter the classroom in a highly engaging manner. Most larger communities have an American Bar Association affiliate. These folks are often willing to come into the classroom to help teachers prepare students for a mock trial. Most states have a state bar association that has materials and resources. The ACLU and Anti-Defamation League usually are happy to provide resources to teachers interested in law-related education. The Center for Civic Education, 5146 Douglas Fir Road, Calabasas, CA 91302, 818-340-9320, has a host of effective and interesting materials at all grade levels. Call and ask for a catalog.

Data Disks

A graphic organizer my kids like is the data disk. Cut a circle from a piece of 12" × 18" paper. Draw segments. I start with six and move to eight later in the year. My kids use these disks for data collection. Because of the limited space, they can't copy their data word for word. I encourage them to write just the facts. To make it clearer what the facts are, I often instruct them to leave out capital letters, ending punctuation, and encourage them to use hyphens between the facts. Whether we are doing data disks on explorers, endangered species, or characteristics of a culture, data disks help students identify and categorize facts, sequence events, and compare and contrast across the classroom.

Time Lines

A traditional social studies skill, time lines also help students with categorizing, sequencing, and organizing data. I always start out with my kids' lives, walking them through construction of their own time lines. Often for my kids, we have to begin with a homework assignment: Go home and find out ten things that have happened to you since you were born and when they happened. (Be sure to give them time to share with peers when they come back!) I set up the time line mathematically, based on the size of paper I have. The kids copy it and then write in their life events. Sometimes I move on to the Yakima Indian Time Ball, a Native American time line to provide a kinesthetic cultural experience. When my students read biographies

214

the rest of the year, one of the requirements they meet is constructing a time line of the main character's life. We also construct time lines of the past month or quarter, trimester or semester. This technique is especially helpful for third and fourth graders, providing an understandable context for time lines.

Musicals

Putting on a musical is a lot of work but can be very rewarding. Take last year for instance. We did a musical called *The Burley Crew*. It was about Lewis and Clark's expedition to Oregon. This year we did one called *How the West Was Really Won*, featuring events from about 1800 to 1870. As the kids learned the songs and worked together (all four of our fifth-grade classes), they were also practicing exemplary social studies skills. The kids were immersed in the topic.

Clapping, Singing, Rapping, Moving to Music

Bring music into your social studies classroom. Inviting kids to create their own rhythms for remembering facts, events, or concepts is very empowering. I use the old *Schoolhouse Rock* series to encourage my kids to do their own thing. Working with the music teacher at my school, we also try to coordinate studies so that the kids are learning about American composers in music from the same period we are focusing on in the classroom, or they are learning songs associated with certain periods (pioneers, railroad, Civil War, and so forth). If you don't have a music teacher, try bringing in tapes or CDs of the music of the period. Libraries often have them for checking out, parents may send in some treasures from personal collections.

Songs About Issues/Folk Songs

Songs have often led or described important historical movements, such as "We Shall Overcome" for the civil rights movement. I think it's important for our students to know the song, and the emotional and intellectual forces behind it. Whether the teacher, the music teacher, or a community person shares this information with the kids is immaterial, but I do think it is an important and often neglected piece of social studies knowledge.

Ethnic Songs

Whenever we are studying a particular culture, I try to find music representative of that culture. Our public library has a pretty good selection and sometimes I put an "all call" out to the kids' parents. Just playing the music in the morning when the kids come in, putting it on during transition times, and having it in the background during lunch provides a bridge to appreciating the diverse cultures. I try to find both traditional and contemporary music of the culture being studied so the kids don't build musical stereotypes.

Color-Coding Work

Color coding work is a useful strategy, especially for third and fourth graders. Whether the students are following the trails of early explorers or identifying mountains, plains, and rivers on a map, color coding helps kids develop discrimination skills used in reading.

Graphs and Charts

Both reading and creating graphs are integral segments of social studies skills. Being able to analyze, interpret, and discern the validity of studies, surveys, and other pictorial representations of information is an important part of the social studies milieu. I seldom teach the graphs unit in math. Instead, I use the social studies text and we practice reading and analyzing graphs found there. Then we move on to newspapers and magazines, looking at sample sizes, questions asked, and data retrieved. Finally, we move to the survey activity previously described, and the kids create their own questionnaires about topics they are interested in, sample an identified population at school, and analyze their data. The last challenge is to create a graph indicating their results. It's great fun!

Mandalas and Coats of Arms

Using graphics to learn certainly isn't new. Think back to cave art, long before alphabets were invented. But in American education, there seems to be a trend that the older kids get, the less visual representation they need to do. Try linking the word with the symbol to help all ages create powerful metaphors. Mandalas are an ancient idea of the circular shape with a number of elements inside the circle creating a whole. Coats of arms are a western representation of a similar idea. See Fran Claggett's book, *Drawing Your Own Conclusions: Graphic Strategies for Reading, Writing, and Thinking* (Heinemann) for more information.

Simulations

Create your own tools in a simulation of pioneer days or ancient times. Capture cultural characteristics of medieval society for a day in your classroom, or give your kids time to create a space colony of the future. Encourage the kids to create miniscenes (slice-of-life views) to demonstrate their understanding of a novel that connects to the period of time being studied, a culture being learned, or a person who made a difference. These scenes, for many teachers, have come out of the shoebox and now take on many forms and use an assortment of materials.

Quilts

Making quilts fits many periods in history (colonial, westward expansion, immigration) and many cultures around the world. Over the years my students have made real quilts from scratch, with the help of interested parents. As their inexperienced hands deal with threading needles and getting their running stitch just right, the kids begin to appreciate the skill, patience, and hard word it takes to make a quilt. We have also done many different kinds of paper quilts. One of my favorite is for the kids to illustrate cardboard patches based on a theme, perhaps the Constitution, the Civil War, or geographic landmarks around the world. Using a paper punch, I punch two to four holes around each edge of each patch. Using yarn, the kids then sew the patches together, making a colorful and informational quilt. A third kind of quilt my kids have made is a memory quilt. These quilts are personal, drawn on a single piece of paper that is divided into squares and usually reflect activities we've studied over a school year.

Usually created in June, these memory quilts accompany my kids as they move on to middle school.

Posters Presenting the Book

Students can create a poster advertising any book, showing key scenes or scenes they think will entice potential readers. They can also make a poster that communicates the essence of the book. My kids like creating posters as if the book they've read is a movie.

Acting Out Scenes from the Book

Students can work in small groups to present key scenes from any book. This can be as formal or informal as desired. Several groups can coordinate a series of scenes as an option.

Designing Clothing That Would Fit the Time and Place of the Story

Costuming actually conveys quite a bit of information. Students who are interested in clothing and fashion can design and/or create costumes that would be appropriate for the characters in the story they are reading. Researching and designing the clothing is plenty of work; I don't ask students or their parents to make the clothing.

What Happens Next

Students write the next chapter (the chapter after the book ends), telling what happens next in the lives of the characters. This is the scene beyond "happily ever after." What happens when Johnny Tremain goes home after the Revolutionary War? What happens after Sam in *Across Five Aprils* becomes a father? Students imagine the logical next piece of the story and present it, either as a play or in written form.

Rewrite a Scene or Chapter from the Point of View of One of the Characters

This is a flexible exercise that can be simple or complex. The task is to take a minor character, or the "bad guy," and have him or her tell the story from his or her own perspective. Tom Stoppard did this in his play, *Rosencranz and Guildenstern Are Dead*, taking two minor characters from *Hamlet* and focusing his play on them. *The True Story of the Three Little Pigs* is a well-known, elementary version of the same exercise. The scenes can be acted out or simply written.

Cartoon Sequence Showing Major Events of the Story

Take six, eight, or more panels to tell the major events of a story in cartoon form. The accent should be on accuracy rather than on drawing skill, but the students should take time with their drawings.

Book Talk

Students present a book to others with a recommendation to read it or not, and why. This can take anywhere from two to ten minutes, and should emphasize what the reader thinks is important, and what you require them to include. This can be done in small groups or with the whole class.

Painting or Drawing

Students create a drawing or painting that depicts a crucial scene from a book. This assignment is self-explanatory, though the students should make it clear why they have chosen certain scenes.

Town Meetings About an Issue or Situation Raised in the Book

Identify a controversial topic that is part of a novel or short story the students are reading, and hold a town meeting about it. Make sure that significant characters from the story are present, and that all relevant viewpoints are heard from.

Interview or Talk Show

Students conduct a talk-show scene, interviewing Abraham Lincoln or one or more of the pioneers after the traumatic events of their encounters on the Oregon Trail. Model a talk show or news interview in format.

Poems

Students can write poems in response to a book they have just read. Read several poems to your students as models. Some kids think all poems have to rhyme. Try structural poetry with them, like cinquains, poems for two voices, or biography poems.

Letter to the Author, Responding to the Book

This is a real-world activity that often brings a reply from the author, assuming he or she is still living. Students write to the author, communicating their own reactions and any questions they might have for the author.

Letter to Someone Who Might be Interested in Reading the Book

Students write a letter to someone else explaining why he or she might or might not want to read this book. The students must use examples from the book and from class discussions and study to support their position.

Composing a Song or Songs on the Themes of the Story

Encourage students to compose their own music. Often the music teacher will help or loan instruments. One of my colleague's students composed a whole symphony, using instruments they made, to express their feelings about old-growth forests.

Investigating a Real World Parallel to the Book

Students might investigate animal testing and experimentation after reading Robert C. O'Brien's Mrs. Frisby and the Rats of NIHM, for example. They might take some real-world action as a part of their study, such as writing a letter to their local paper, or to a relevant company or agency.

Mapping

Have students create maps of the classroom, of the school, of the neighborhood in which the school is located. One of a pair of students places a marker on a specific point on the room map (or a map of the school). His or her partner places an object on the corresponding point in the room (or school). The challenge is to place the marker in the school at the exact place indicated on the map. The reverse of the previous activity: One student places an object in the room and the partner identifies the corresponding point on a map.

Mapping the Same Place from Different Points of View

Students map the room from the front (teacher's view), from the sides, from the ceiling, from the back center. How does the map change?

Another Perspective

Bring in a map that has other countries at the center, and one that has the United States "upside down," a natural consequence to having Australia, for example, at the center. These maps are sold at various map stores or you can order from World Eagle, 111 King Street, Littleton, MA 01460-1527, or call 800-854-8273 and e-mail is info@worldeagle.com. Have the students create a map that turns the world upside down, so that they realize there is no such thing as "upside down" in space.

Models of the Earth

Go from the outside in, through to its core, creating the earth from various colors of clay and bits of stuff. Try including bones, rocks, and other things that would be present.

Playing with Scale

Work with extremes, making things suddenly small or large. How would students perceive and map the room from their new size (as ants, elephants)? Teach your kids how to use grid lines to enlarge or decrease size to draw reduced or enlarged products. This activity is a good activity before teaching latitude and longitude.

Imaginary Island or Country Map

Have the kids be the only one who has ever seen this particular place, so they can decide to include whatever they wish. They must create a key, a scale, a compass rose, and other map features. *The Once upon a Time Map Book* (see bibliography for Chapter 2), provides some great models.

Decide How to Decide

Make it clear to your class which decisions are yours alone, and have regular meetings to decide things you are willing to have them take on.

Leadership Skills

Give each student an hour (or half an hour) to lead the class in some activity. It is for the student to decide what happens during that time, although you can state contingencies (that is, the normal school day must keep going). Plan a session with the student before to help ensure it will be successful.

Class Council

Establish a class council for dealing with class issues such as who will do classroom jobs, how to resolve disputes, and how to give service to the school.

Room Name

My students love to name our room each year. The name is often a foreshadowing of goals we hope to accomplish or how we want to be treated: Paradise Island, Spaceship Earth, Imagination Express.

Recipes

Gather recipes from various countries, including information about the ingredients that are used in the recipes. Look for similarities around the world. Look at supply and demand, what droughts and hurricanes do to food supplies, where there is abundance and where there is not enough. Kids may use the Internet to discover recipes that are unfamiliar, or staples common to a region. Try an international potluck and invite the parents. Use recipes to teach fractions.

Readers Theater

Students create readers theater from material they have researched. The material is presented either to the other members of the class or to other classes.

Newspapers and Newscasts
About a Particular Time or Issue

My classes have created newspapers "from" the Revolutionary War era, the Civil War, the Harlem Renaissance, Shakespeare's England, and other times and places. Students cover major stories, "interview" famous people, review plays (of Shakespeare, for example), and offer other stories appropriate to the time and place. Also try the other side of the story; for example, a Coast Salish Indian watching the first white settlers move into Puget Sound.

Political Cartoons

Students create political cartoons emphasizing a point of view on a particular issue or theme. They might also create a pair of cartoons, each presenting a different point of view on the same issue.

Historical Interviews

Students interview each other as particular historical figures, preparing appropriate questions and answers to bring out information their interview subject has to share with the class. Students might also prepare their own speeches as a historical figure or memorize a famous speech of a historical figure.

Photo Essays

Students compile photographs into an essay or documentary that makes a statement about a relevant topic. Kids can do the same things with cutout pictures from magazines, putting them in poster form or collage form, writing a narration, and videotaping the pictures as the narration is being spoken.

Student Study Groups

Students decide to study a topic that is of common interest to them. They are responsible for defining their goals and objectives and for communicating what they have found.

Nonwritten Reports

Students prepare visual displays, models, dioramas, collages, costumes, art pieces, or something else that communicates what they have discovered from their research.

Journals of Your Studies

Students keep journals as the class moves through a unit of study. They record information, questions, their own reactions and responses. Their responses might be entirely self-defined and generated, or replies to teacher prompts.

FIGURE 5–2 *Cassie*

Assessment Possibilities

Here is a list of projects you can assign for assessement:

Create a piece of art that demonstrates . . .

Invent a board or card game to demonstrate . . .

Use an overhead projector to teach . . .

Explain how the music of a song is similar to . . .

Collect and present songs about . . .

Indicate the rhythmical patterns in . . .

Use storytelling to explain . . .

Create a talk-show radio program about . . .

Invent slogans for . . .

Make a calendar of . . .

Describe symmetry in . . .

Translate . . . into a mathematical formula.

Create a personal analogy for . . .

Explain the purpose in studying . . .

Describe how you feel about . . .

Create and implement group rules for . . .

Use a conflict management strategy to . . .

Use a telecommunication program to reach . . .

Create a movement or sequence of movements to explain . . .

Invent a floor game of . . .

Design a product for . . .

Professional Books

AYERS, WILLIAM. 1993. *To Teach*. New York: Teachers College.

This educator writes about what really happens in a classroom. He is very sensitive to meeting the needs of all children, and writes about how he struggles with this in his own classroom. He writes in a very personal way about his own situation, but he is clearly dealing with issues that are common to all of us in the classroom.

Burke, Kay. 1994. *The Mindful School: How to Assess Authentic Learning.* Palatine, IL: IRI/Skylight Publishing.

A teacher-friendly manual to assist us with matching assessment to the way we teach and kids learn. Clear text, graphic examples, and models that can be put in place in our classrooms tomorrow are provided. Learn about strategies to use for portfolios, performances, and projects. Check possibilities for assessing learning logs and journals. Find guidelines for creating your own tests or using the information from standardized tests in a beneficial way. Discover the value of observation checklists, graphic organizers, and interviews. Look at the issues around grading.

Campbell, Bruce, Linda Campbell, and Dee Dickinson. 1992. *Teaching and Learning Through the Multiple Intelligences.* Stanwood, WA: New Horizons for Learning.

A thoughtful guide to putting the multiple intelligences into practice in the classroom. Whether a teacher is new to the theory of multiple intelligences or has been "using the idea" for years, this book widens the options and stretches the ways our students can show they are smart. I especially like the menu selection for possibilities for assessment, some of which can be found at the end of this chapter.

Culham, Ruth. 1998. *Picture Books: An Annotated Bibliography with Activities for Teaching Writing,* 5th ed. Portland, OR: Northwest Regional Educational Laboratory.

Although this book is organized by six writing traits: ideas and content, organization, voice, word choice, sentence fluency, and conventions, it is easy to find books that also connect to social studies, science, and health content. Over fifty teacher lessons are included for grades K–14. It's a helpful way to begin deliberately integrating writing skills with content across the curriculum.

Delpit, Lisa. 1995. *Other People's Children.* New York: New Press.

Lisa Delpit offers a significant look at the education of African American children. She looks at the alternative and progressive approaches to education and challenges some of their basic assumptions with reference to students of color. She offers the notion that many students of color have to learn how to "speak" the language of power, that they have to learn the rules of success in their society. Ms. Delpit challenges some long-held notions of education in a very convincing manner. She offers some insightful and practical observations that have changed how I approach my own work.

FOGARTY, ROBIN. 1991. *The Mindful School: How to Integrate Curricula.* Palatine, IL: IRI/Skylight Publishing.

The author clearly and graphically identifies ten different ways curricula can be integrated. From nested, webbed, and threaded to immersed and networked, she helps us all see that there truly is more than one way to integrate our teaching and our students' learning. This resource gives teachers not only a vision of how to integrate but also provides choices from many different ways to organize integration within our classrooms.

HALL, SUSAN. 1994. *Using Picture Storybooks to Teach Literary Devices: Recommended Books for Children and Young Adults.* Phoenix, AZ: Oryx Press.

From alliteration, allusion, atmosphere, and analogy to satire, simile, stereotype, theme, tone, and understatement, literary devices are identified and taught through picture storybooks. Each literary device has a eight to twelve sources listed that teachers can use as a model for the device. This book can help teachers move away from the basal teacher's manuals and begin to explore how to teach from a broader, often more engaging, literature platform. In addition to an annotation for each source cited, an example or suggestion of how it might be used in included.

GARDNER, HOWARD. 1999. *The Disciplined Mind: What All Students Should Understand.* New York: Simon & Schuster.

Gardner moves into new territory as he explores what an educated person should be and how such an education can be achieved for all students. He presents the argument that the purpose of a K–12 education should be to help students understand truth, beauty, and goodness. He suggests six different educational pathways that together could lead to satisfying most people's concern for student learning and understanding. This would be a great "book club" choice for you and your colleagues.

GILBERT, ANNE GREEN. 1977. *Teaching the Three Rs Through Movement Experience.* Minneapolis, MN: Burgess Publishing Company.

A classic that belongs on every teacher's shelf! Long before kinesthetic learners were recognized as a large portion of our student population, Anne Green Gilbert was urging teachers to include kinesthetic learning strategies in the classroom. Her ideas are as fresh and as necessary today as they were twenty years ago.

HARVEY, STEPHANIE. 1998. *Nonfiction Matters: Reading, Writing, and Research in Grades 3–8*. York, ME: Stenhouse Publishing.

This book offers teachers the tools to help students explore nonfiction and dig deep to reach a more complete understanding of the real world and report those insights in a compelling manner. It's full of practical suggestions to bring nonfiction into your curriculum.

HICKEY, M. GAIL. 1999. *Bringing History Home: Local and Family History Projects for Grades K–6*. Needham Heights, MA: Allyn & Bacon.

A wonderfully helpful guide for classroom teachers who are interested in exploring their own communities and inviting their students become both content and investigator. I especially like Hickey's suggestions for creating classroom almanacs. She focuses on two main kinds of history: family history and community and local history.

IRVIN, JUDITH L., et al. 1995. *Enhancing Social Studies Through Literacy Strategies*. Washington, D.C.: National Council for the Social Studies.

A lean, but helpful professional bulletin, this book concentrates on powerful ways to integrate language arts and literacy skills with social studies content. From building vocabulary and conceptual knowledge through critical thinking and deliberate linking of literature and history, the authors not only show how to connect the two disciplines, but identify potential pitfalls.

JOHNSTONE, KEITH. 1984. *Impro*. New York: Theater Arts Books.

This is an extraordinary book written by an extraordinary educator. Johnstone is the founder of Theatresports, and has developed techniques for helping improvisers free themselves up to create effective theater. Johnstone is an educator who can communicate the essence of education, and who can offer wise words about the damage done by traditional schooling. I use this book as a regular reminder that education is most effective if it is inspiring students and teacher alike to be more alive, more creative, and more in touch with their world.

KEMPER, DAVE, et al. 1995. *Writers Express: A Handbook for Young Writers, Thinkers and Learners*. Wilmington, MA: D.C. Heath.

The best handbook written for intermediate learners that we've seen. It provides models, assistance, and rules for all the writing exercises that our kids are supposed to be able to do. The same company also has the books for middle-school writers and primary writers. Just call their toll-free number, 800-289-4490, to get a catalog and current prices. Every teacher should have one of these. (There is a student version and a teacher's manual. We just use the student version.) It's even better and a much more efficient use of time if you can get a classroom set. This single book will help you integrate writing with content (and meet statewide standards) more effectively than any other source we know.

KIELBURGER, CRAIG. 1998. *Free the Children*. New York: HarperCollins.

Craig Kielburger is the young man (now fifteen) who began an organization devoted to ending child-labor abuse around the world. He began his work at age twelve, and has traveled the world on behalf of children. His organization is run by children and young adults, and his story is incredible.

KOHL, HERBERT. 1994. *I Won't Learn from You*. New York: Teachers College.

Kohl offers a number of insights in this little book about why some students make choices that seem, on the surface, to be not in their best interests. A useful analysis about why some students, even very bright ones, don't seem to learn at school. Mr. Kohl is very sensitive to issues of race, power, and gender in the classroom, and has useful insights about why we so often fail to reach children.

KOHN, ALFIE. 1993. *Punished by Rewards*. Boston: Houghton Mifflin.

Kohn challenges the notion of extrinsic rewards, teaching children to respond to adult praise or disapproval. He argues that we are training children to ignore their own interests and values in an attempt to fit in and to please others. He suggests that we should help students to take more responsibility for their work and for assessing their own work and learning.

KOZOL, JONATHAN. 1992. *Savage Inequalities*. New York: HarperCollins.

———. 1996. *Amazing Grace*. New York: HarperCollins.

Jonathan Kozol has written many books about education and the society in which our schools function, and they are all provocative and wise. *Savage Inequalities* identifies many of the funding problems that challenge our inner-city schools. *Amazing Grace* looks at the inner-city world of some of our students. Mr. Kozol writes with passion, with wisdom, and with his focus clearly on who children are, what they need, and how we can meet those needs.

LEVINE, DAVID, ROBERT LOWE, BOB PETERSON, and RITA TENORIO, eds. 1995. *Rethinking Schools: An Agenda for Change.* New York: New Press.

This book is put out by the educators who produce the journal *Rethinking Schools*. The journal was created by educators in the Milwaukee Public Schools, and regularly deals with the challenges of finding justice in the public schools (especially urban public schools). This book features essays on race, gender, community, educational reform, testing, choice and vouchers, and more, offering strong analysis, commentary, and information about the issues.

LINDQUIST, TARRY. 1995. *Seeing the Whole Through Social Studies.* Portsmouth, NH: Heinemann.

This book grew out of my twelve-year exploration of ways to network knowledge, skills, and teaching strategies across the curriculum using social studies as the framework. My story is about reorganizing curriculum and choosing instructional strategies to make learning integrative, meaningful, value-based, active, and challenging for both students and teachers.

———. 1997. *Ways That Work: Putting Social Studies Standards into Practice.* Portsmouth, NH: Heinemann.

This is an idea book. It models several different ways social studies content can be organized in elementary and middle-school classrooms. Each chapter identifies a specific standard and goal, presents strategies to help you achieve that goal, outlines how to put the strategies in place, describes essential skills you can help your kids develop, suggests ways you can incorporate other subject areas, especially language arts and literature, and presents proven assessment techniques.

LONDON, PETER. 1989. *No More Second Hand Art.* Boston: Shambhala.

Peter London is an artist and teacher who reminds the reader that art is about making meaning, not making pretty. People have used the arts to communicate with nature, with their gods, with the major forces in their lives. The book encourages me to help my students do things of real value in the classroom rather than to settle for activities that look good but have little meaning.

NATIONAL COUNCIL FOR THE SOCIAL STUDIES. 1994. *Curriculum Standards for Social Studies: Expectations of Excellence.* Washington, D.C.: National Council for the Social Studies.

Developed by the National Council for the Social Studies, this handbook provides guidance to teachers when selecting themes to teach and performance expectations for students in the field of social studies. Also, essential skills are identified and a critical discussion about what makes excellent social studies in today's classrooms is provided.

OHANIAN, SUSAN. 1999. *One Size Fits Few: The Folly of Educational Standards*. Portsmouth, NH: Heinemann.

This brief, irreverent book reminds us to trust ourselves and do what we know is best for kids. Too many of us beat ourselves up because we are caught between teaching kids the way we know we should and teaching to "the test." Ohanian's look at the pro-standards movement gives us permission to teach kids, not standards.

OPITZ, MICHAEL, and TIMOTHY V. RASINSKI. 1998. *Goodbye Round Robin: 25 Effective Oral Reading Strategies*. Portsmouth, NH: Heinemann.

While it is true that we most often read silently, there are times when oral reading is needed, too. This book shares several effective and efficient ways to use oral reading in the classroom for maximum benefit as well as how oral reading fits into a total, balanced reading program.

PALEY, VIVIAN. 1992. *You Can't Say You Can't Play*. Cambridge, MA: Harvard University Press.

This wonderful little book takes on the fundamental issues of the classroom (what should be taught, what is important, how do we make decisions, how do we listen to each other) in a clear, simple style. Paley really listens to children, and writes in a manner that is both engaging and powerful in its clarity.

POSTMAN, NEIL. 1985. *Amusing Ourselves to Death*. New York: Penguin.

Neal Postman offers a critique of media, especially the news media. His work is very useful in helping students to become more media literate. He identifies many of the pressures and influences that conspire to keep us from being well informed, and has some suggestions for how we can become more literate consumers of news and media.

RAPHAEL, TAFFY E., et al. 1997. *Book Club: A Literature-Based Curriculum*. Andover, MA: Small Planet Communications, Inc.

Want to move away from literature circles in your intermediate classroom? Try book clubs! Some of the best conversations and real kid-centered talk has occurred in my classroom when I've used the organization and ideas from this book. Research based and classroom tested, this teacher's handbook opens the door to higher-level thinking, reflective writing, and critical conversations about what matters to young readers. Highly recommended!

Selwyn, Douglas. 1993. *Living History in the Classroom*. Tuscon, AZ: Zephyr Press.

This book is for readers who are looking for ways to activate their classrooms, especially through the theater arts. Capitalizing on literature connections to social studies and how they might lead students to greater understanding of history and enthusiasm for social studies through role-playing, miming, mock trials, and movement activities, Selwyn reassures the new teacher that these strategies are not only effective, but fun for the teacher and the students!

————. 1995. *Arts & Humanities in the Social Studies*. Washington, D.C.: National Council for the Social Studies.

A professional bulletin, this book briefly introduces the reader to learning through the arts, specifically using theater in the classroom and combining creative writing with literature and content from the social studies.

Smith, Shelley J., et al. 1996. *Intrigue of the Past: A Teacher's Activity Guide for Fourth Through Seventh Grade*. Washington, D.C.: United States Department of the Interior, Bureau of Land Management.

A guide to teaching archaeology in the classroom, this manual is divided into three major sections: "Fundamental Concepts," "The Process of Archaeology," and "Issues in Archaeology." Specific lessons are provided that can be used as is or shaped to fit individual classroom explorations. The website address is: www.co.blm.gov/ahc/projectarch.htm.

Spolin, Viola. 1983. *Improvisation for the Theater: A Handbook of Teaching and Directing Techniques*. Evanston, IL: Northwestern University Press.

This is the mother lode of improvisational theater techniques, a sourcebook for improvisers around the world. Spolin's exercises are easily adaptable to kindergarten classrooms through college. Many of these exercises emphasize communication and connection with others, and allow you and the students to explore setting, character, attitudes, and point of view.

Wiggins, Grant, and Jay McTighe. 1998. *Understanding by Design*. Alexandria, VA: Association for Supervision and Curriculum Development.

Wiggins and McTighe offer an alternative template for designing integrated units across the curriculum. We particularly like their "working backwards" approach to developing curriculum. Their WHERE acronym triggers helpful teacher checkpoints.

ZARNOWSKI, MYRA and ARLENE F. GALLAGHER. 1993. *Children's Literature & Social Studies: Selecting and Using Notable Books in the Classroom.* Washington, D.C.: National Council for the Social Studies.

Although the books cited as resources may be more classic than contemporary, the teaching strategies shared are top-notch. Part one focuses on selecting books for classroom instruction. Part two highlights using books in classroom instruction, including talk shows, literature sets, literature packets, and literature folders to foster social studies learning.

ZEMELMAN, STEVEN, et al. 1998. *Best Practice: New Standards for Teaching and Learning in America's Schools*, 2nd ed. Portsmouth, NH: Heinemann.

A wonderful aid in helping teachers look at their own practice and determine which attitudes, behaviors, strategies, and activities work best in today's classrooms. Practical suggestions for incorporating instructional excellence are provided as well as state-of-the-art descriptions of progressive teaching in six areas: reading, writing, mathematics, science, social studies, and the arts. Whether you're affirmed in what you are already doing, or want to be informed about practices you hadn't considered, this book will help you create a classroom where all children can learn in a student-centered, experiential, democratic, collaborative, and challenging environment.

ZINN, HOWARD. 1995. *A People's History of the United States.* New York: Harper Perennial.

This is an extraordinary book written by a professor emeritus of history at Boston University. Professor Zinn has taken the traditional United States history and turned it on its ear. His mission is to make sure that the voices and people who are usually unheard, or presented in an unfavorable light, get equal time and respect, and then some. Dr. Zinn challenges many traditional versions of history and his text leads to many thought-provoking conversations and assignments. The text is aimed at adults, but the ideas are certainly relevant for any classroom.

Magazines

Creative Classroom is a magazine published six times per year, dedicated to supporting creativity and integration in the classroom.

Standard features include "Putting It All Together," practical and innovative ways to deal with those difficult topics and concerns in our classrooms and support for integrative units that provide models and materials that can be used in the classroom tomorrow. Technology, new books, and thoughtful discussions by teachers about teaching and learning today. Subscription rate is $19.97 per year. Check www.creativeclassroom.com for further information, or write to 149 Fifth Ave., 12th Floor, New York, NY 10010.

Social Education is the official journal of the National Council for the Social Studies, published seven times a year. Membership in the National Council for the Social Studies is open to any person or institution interested in the social studies. Comprehensive membership dues are $65. Regular membership dues are $50. Student/retiree membership dues are $27. All memberships include the newsletter, *The Social Studies Professional*. Members can choose as a benefit either a full subscription to *Social Education* or a full subscription to *Social Studies and the Young Learner*. The annual subscription rate, included in membership dues, is $35. To join NCSS, write to PO Box 79078, Baltimore, MD 21279-0078 or call 800-296-7840. Visit NCSS online at www.ncss.org.

Teaching Tolerance is a magazine mailed twice a year to educators at no charge. It is published by the Southern Poverty Law Center, a nonprofit legal and education foundation. Fostering multicultural education and respect for all peoples, this magazine includes idea exchanges, interesting interviews from multiple perspectives, teaching resources, new books, grant opportunities, and current issues. Send in your name, school, and address to *Teaching Tolerance*, PO Box 548, Montgomery, AL 36177-9621 for your free copy.

Book Links is a publication of the American Library Association. It is designed for teachers, librarians, library media specialists, parents, and other interested adults. *Book Links* publishes bibliographies, essays linking books on a similar theme, retrospective reviews, and other features that keep us current with both recently published books and collections of books on specific topics. It is a bimonthly magazine available for $29.95 per year. Call 630-892-7465 or write to *Book Links*, 50 E. Huron Street, Chicago, IL 60611.

Catalogs

Filmic Archives, a comprehensive selection of educational videos, updates their catalog a couple of times a year. Specializing in videos and CD-ROMs for grades K–8, they feature literature, Newbery winners, language skills, early childhood, science and ecology, space, math, geography, and more. I especially like the social studies topics available, ranging from a regional look at Native Americans to *Johnny Tremain* to *Sounder* and *Roll of Thunder, Hear My Cry*. Inexpensive compared to most video prices, you'll also get same-day service. Call 800-366-1920, fax 203-268-1796 or e-mail at custsrv@filmicarchives.com.

Recorded Books, Inc. is a catalog of over two thousand unabridged, complete audiobooks for grades K–12. These books provide a multisensory or alternative approach to reading. For those teachers who want all their students enriched by reading novels that fit their curriculum content, here's a way to make sure no one is left out. Tape Assisted Reading Programs (TARP) are recognized as effective supports for those kids who haven't yet acquired the reading skills of their peers. It is also a helpful device to use with ESL students. Classics and Spanish titles are also available. Tapes can be rented or purchased. Call 800-638-1304 for a catalog or visit their website at www.recordedbooks.com.

Teacher's Video Company, PO Box ELL-4455, Scottsdale, AZ 85261, offers a catalog of appropriate videos designed for grades three through six for U.S. history, social studies, geography, language arts, math, physical education, art, music, science, and more. Seventh- and eighth-grade teachers, ask for a catalog for your grade level. All videos cost $29.95. Good service and great selection. Ordering by calling 800-262-8837, or fax 602-860-8650.

Plays

Discovery Enterprises, Ltd. at 800-729-1720 publishes a series of low-cost plays for real classrooms of kids (usually twenty-seven to thirty-five roles) on various historical events: *The Underground Railroad*, a play in three acts; *Marching Through Time*, a play about the turn of the century; *The Salem Witch Hunt*, a one-act play; *The First Voyage of Christopher Columbus*; *Working in Darkness*, a play about coal mining; *How the*

West Was Won by Railroad, and so forth. These plays are appropriate for fifth through eighth grades. Call for ordering information and a catalog.

Current Events

Time for Kids is a student periodical published twenty-six times a year from September to May for the classroom rate of $3.95 per student. It's a great way to combine current events with language arts, reading, and writing practice. Helpful teacher hints are provided weekly. For subscription queries, call 800-777-8600. E-mail address is TFK@time.com, or the website is www.timeforkids.com.

Websites

You can find information on an incredible number and range of sites on the World Wide Web, devoted to social studies or social studies-related issues. The sites are listed by topic or area, and offer teachers a solid starting place for tracking down information, primary documents, photographs, and other materials related to virtually anything you are teaching.

American Memory: http://memory.loc.gov/ammem/
    This is the website for the Library of Congress collection, and it is invaluable. It is a wonderful site for photographs, for primary sources, for journals, and information.

CSS Journal: http://www.cssjournal.com/journal/sites.html
    This is a compendium of hundreds of social studies sites on the web.

Center for Civic Education: http://www.civiced.org/
    The Center for Civic education offers resources and materials devoted to issues of citizenship and democracy: "We the People" is one of their programs. They have programs designed to help students understand and appreciate the constitution and our system of government.

ERIC Clearinghouse for Social Studies/Social Science Education: http://www.indiana.edu/ ~ ssdc/eric_chess.htm
    This is a very useful clearinghouse for information about social studies related teaching, with lesson plans and links to many useful sites.

Fairness and Accuracy in Reporting: http://www.fair.org/

    FAIR is an organization that looks toward media with a critical eye. They are concerned with media bias and fairness, and offer good information about media literacy.

Free the Children: http://www.freethechildren.org/index.html

    Free the Children is an organization started by children devoted to taking on the abuses of child labor throughout the world. Craig Kielburger was twelve years old when he became aware of child-labor issues and he has worked with other students to create a worldwide organization that is both inspiring and informative. This site documents child-labor abuses around the world and features efforts being made to stop them. This organization, led by children, shows students what can be done.

H-Net, Humanities and Social Studies Online: http://www.h-net.msu .edu/

    This is the Michigan State University collection of discussion networks and information on a wide range of subjects, including history. I am a member of a number of h-net listserves and find them very useful for making contact with others interested in teaching social studies.

Homework Helper: http://tristate.pgh.net/~pinch13/

    A great homework helper site created by a thirteen-year-old-boy and his dad. They keep the site up to date. It's kid friendly and useful.

International Reading Association: http://www.ira.org and American Library Association: http://www.ala.org

    Two resources on the Internet to help you hook into reading issues, ideas, and skills, bringing them into your classroom are these two sites.

Library of Congress: http://lcweb.loc.gov/exhibits/G.Address/gadrft.html

    One of our favorites, the Library of Congress exhibits of Lincoln's "Gettysburg Address." You can download two drafts in Lincoln's handwriting (plus transcription) that proves to the kids that process writing was being used 130 years ago! You can also download the only photograph we know that was taken of Lincoln while he was speaking at Gettysburg. Other historical events are also available at the Library of Congress site; just type in the address without the portion, "G.Address/gadrft.html."

National Arts Education Association. http://www.naea-reston.org
Links the visitor to state arts organizations.

Music Educators National Conference: http://www.uwec.edu/student/mused
This site will connect you with the lead organization representing various groups involved in music education. Look for helpful bulletins, research news and conference announcements.

National Council for History Education: http://www.history.org/nche/
A source of many links to the teaching of history on a wide range of topics. This is a good place to turn for background information, perspective, and links to many points of view on whatever period of history you are teaching.

National Council for the Social Studies: www.ncss.org
This site is the home page for NCSS. Lesson plans, networks, travel opportunities, research, and teaching techniques are just some of the support available here.

National Council of Teachers of Mathematics: http://www.nctm.org
Keep up to date with materials, events, revisions of standards, and a host of other information.

The National Women's History Project: http://www.nwhp.org/welcome.html
All sorts of assistance is provided in making sure women have an accurate and fair representation in what we teach. Information ranges from ideas and references for teachers through appropriate sites for student research.

National Writing Project: http://www-gse.berkeley.edu
Looking for an outstanding resource on practice, research, and ideas on writing? Try here for support and suggestions.

National Science Teachers Association: http://www.nsta.org
Membership, news, research, and quite a few beneficial bulletins and publications are provided with helpful hints for better science in our classrooms.

New Horizons for Learning: http://www.newhorizons.org/
New Horizons for Learning is an organization focused on how people learn, and has many links to issues ranging from brain research to learning styles to lesson plans.

Notable Children's Trade Books in the Field of Social Studies 1999: www.ncss.org

An annotated list of books that were published the previous year and are written primarily for children in grades K–8. Books on this list were selected because they emphasize human relationships, represent a diversity of groups, and are sensitive to a broad range of cultural experience, present an original theme or a fresh slant on a traditional topic, are easily readable and of high literary quality, have a pleasing format, and when appropriate, illustrations enrich the text. Each book is read by several committee members and books are included on the list by committee assent. The committee is appointed by the National Council for the Social Studies and assembled in cooperation with the Children's Book Council.

Outstanding Science Trade Books for Children, 1999: www.nsta.org/pubs/sc/ostb99.htm

This list is the result of a cooperative project between the National Science Teachers Association and the Children's Book Council. This list is published annually in the March issue of *Science and Children*, the journal devoted to preschool through middle-level science teaching. The list is also available through NSTA's Fax on Demand. This twenty-four-hour touchtone telephone service will prompt you into selecting a form or other material published by NSTA. Call toll free 888-400-NSTA. When prompted, select number 845 to receive a faxed copy of the trade book list.

PBS Online: http://www.pbs.org/

Public Broadcasting offers much support for the programs they present on television. This frequently includes background information, maps, journals, lesson plans, links to other sites, and biographies. Their links and teacher materials to accompany the *Lewis and Clark* program, for example, are superb.

Rethinking Schools: http://www.rethinkingschools.org/

This organization was started by teachers in the Milwaukee school district, and is concerned with issues facing urban education. They "remain firmly committed to equity and to the vision that public education is central to the creation of a humane, caring, multiracial democracy." Their journal is oriented toward addressing issues of substance facing teachers and students in the public schools. It is a wonderful resource. Subscriptions at RSBusiness@aol.com.

The Resource Center of the Americas: www.americas.org

This center creates innovative and challenging curricula and provides other educational tools that build bridges between people throughout the Americas. They have served educators since 1983. In addition to curricula, they also have a project on labor and global economy; a child-labor project; a lending library of eight thousand books, periodicals, and videos; and workshops on the history and culture of Mexican Americans. This site contains a listing of over two thousand books on the Americas. Periodic updates of new resources can also be found on e-mail at bookstore@americas.org.

Social Studies Around the Web: http://www.li.net/~ndonohue/ssus.html
This is Nancy Donohue's list of favorite sites on the World Wide Web. She is a teacher who has amassed a huge list of favorites. She has arranged the list by topic, and it can be intimidating because there are so many of them, but it is well organized and easy to navigate.

ZNET: http://www.lbbs.org/
This site comes from South End Press, which publishes Z magazine, with in-depth articles and information on a range of issues, from a liberal point of view. Their articles offer analysis that is often different from that of mainstream newspapers or magazines, which can be very useful when helping students to understand the importance of point of view and bias in social studies.

The National Council for the Social Studies Thematic Standards

Following is a list of the ten thematic standards developed by NCSS:

1. Culture: Who are we, how do we live our lives, who are other people, and how do they live their lives, and how do we deal with each other?
2. People, places and the environment: Where do we live, how are we shaped by the places we live, and how do we affect the environments in which we live?
3. Time, continuity and change: What is our story over time? Where have we come from, how did we get here, and where are we headed?

4. Individual development and identity: Who are we as individuals, and how do we find our places as individuals and as members of the larger community?

5. Individuals, groups, and institutions: How do we, as individuals, function as members of various groups and institutions within society; how is society shaped by those various groups, including families, schools, religions, business systems, and the media, and how do we, as individuals, shape our institutions?

6. Power, governance, and authority: What is power, who has it (and why), and how does that change over time? How do societies organize themselves, and how do they govern themselves? What happens to those without power?

7. Production, distribution, and consumption: How do societies generate what they need, how do they generate wealth, and how do they distribute that wealth to its members? Why is there a large income gap between those who own the production process and those who carry out the process?

8. Science, technology, and society: How does science and technology affect how we live, how we produce and consume, and how we view the world?

9. Global connections: How do societies see themselves within the world community, and in what ways do they make connections to that larger community? How does what happens in the United States change lives in countries around the world, and vice versa?

10. Civic ideals and practices: How do we live as members of a society? What does right living mean, and how do we function as productive citizens of a society?

Appendix A
The Essential Social Studies Skills

The Essential Social Studies Skills

Acquiring Information

A. **READING SKILLS**
1. Comprehension
   Read to get literal meaning.
   Use chapter and section headings, topic sentences, and summary
     sentences to select main idea.
   Differentiate main and subordinate ideas.
   Select passages that are pertinent to the topic studied.
   Interpret what is read by drawing inferences.
   Detect cause-and-effect relationships.
   Distinguish between fact and opinion; recognize propaganda.
   Recognize author bias.
   Use picture clues and picture captions to aid comprehension.
   Use literature to enrich meaning.
   Read for a variety of purposes: critically, analytically, to predict outcomes,
     to answer questions, to form an opinion, to skim for facts.
   Read various forms of printed material: books, magazines, newspapers,
     directories, schedules, journals.
2. Vocabulary
   Use usual word-attack skills: sight recognition, phonetic analysis,
     structural analysis.
   Use context clues to gain meaning.
   Use appropriate sources to gain meaning of essential terms and
     vocabulary: glossary, dictionary, text, word lists.
   Recognize and understand an increasing number of social studies terms.
3. Rate of Reading
   Adjust speed to suit purpose.
   Adjust rate of reading to difficulty of material.

B. **STUDY SKILLS**
1. Find Information
   Use various parts of a book (index, table of contents, and so forth).
   Use key words, letters on volumes, index, and cross-references to find
     information.
   Evaluate sources of information: print, visual, electronic.
   Use appropriate source of information.
   Use the community as a resource.

---

2. Arrange Information in Usable Form
Make outline of topic.
Prepare summaries.
Make time lines.
Take notes.
Keep records.
Use italics, margin notes, and footnotes.
Listen for information.
Follow directions.
Write reports and research papers.
Prepare a bibliography.

C. **REFERENCE AND INFORMATION-SEARCH SKILLS**
1. Use the Library
Use print and electronic catalogs to locate books.
Use indexes such as *Reader's Guide to Period Literature*.
Use public-library telephone information service.
2. Special References
Almanacs
Encyclopedias
Dictionaries
Indexes
Government publications
Microfiche
Periodicals
News sources: newspapers, newsmagazines, TV, radio, videotapes,
artifacts
3. Maps, Globes, Graphics
Use map and globe-reading skills.
Orient a map and note directions.
Locate places on map and globe.
Use scale and compute distances.
Interpret map symbols and visualize what they mean.
Compare maps and make inferences.
Express relative location.
Interpret graphs.
Detect bias in visual material.
Interpret social and political messages of cartoons.
Interpret history through artifacts.
4. Community Resources
Use sources of information in the community.
Conduct interviews of individuals in the community.
Use community newspapers.

D. **TECHNICAL SKILLS UNIQUE TO ELECTRONIC DEVICES**
1. Computer
Operate a computer using prepared instructional or reference programs.

Operate a computer to enter and retrieve information gathered from a variety of sources.
2. Telephone and Television Information Networks
Access information through networks.

Organizing and Using Information

A. THINKING SKILLS
 1. Classify Information
 Identify relevant factual material.
 Sense relationship between items of factual information.
 Group data in categories according to appropriate criteria.
 Place information in proper sequence.
  Order of occurrence
  Order of importance
 Place data in tabular form: charts, graphs, illustrations.
 2. Interpret Information
 State relationships between categories of information.
 Note cause-and-effect relationships.
 Draw inferences from factual materials.
 Predict likely outcomes based on factual information.
 Recognize the value dimension of interpreting factual information.
 Recognize instances in which more than one interpretation of factual material is valid.
 3. Analyze Information
 Form a simple organization of key ideas related to a topic.
 Separate a topic into major components according to appropriate criteria.
 Examine critically relationships between and among elements of a topic.
 Detect bias in data presented in various forms: graphics, tabular, visual, print.
 Compare and contrast credibility of differing accounts of the same event.
 4. Summarize Information
 Extract significant ideas from supporting illustrative details.
 Combine critical concepts into a statement of conclusions based on information.
 Restate major ideas of a complex topic in concise form.
 Form opinion based on critical examination of relevant information.
 State hypothesis for further study.
 5. Synthesize Information
 Propose a new plan of operation, create a new system, or devise a futuristic scheme based on available information.
 Reinterpret events in terms of what *might* have happened, and show the likely effects on subsequent events.
 Present visually (chart, graph, diagram, model, and so forth) information extracted from print.
 Prepare a research paper that requires a creative solution to a problem.
 Communicate orally and in writing.
 6. Evaluate Information
 Determine whether or not information is pertinent to the topic.

Estimate the adequacy of the information.
Test the validity of the information, using such criteria as source, objectivity, technical correctness, currency.

B. DECISION-MAKING SKILLS

Identify a situation in which a decision is required.
Secure needed factual information.
Recognize the values implicit in the situation and the issues that flow from them.
Identify alternative courses of action and predict likely consequences of each.
Make decision based on the data obtained.
Take action to implement decision.

C. METACOGNITIVE SKILLS

Select appropriate strategy to solve a problem.
Self-monitor one's thinking process.

Interpersonal Relationships and Social Participation

A. PERSONAL SKILLS

Express personal convictions.
Communicate own beliefs, feelings, and convictions.
Adjust own behavior to fit the dynamics of various groups and situations.
Recognize mutual relationship between human beings in satisfying one another's needs.

B. GROUP INTERACTION SKILLS

Contribute to the development of a supportive climate in groups.
Participate in making rules and guidelines for group life.
Serve as a leader or a follower.
Assist in setting goals for the group.
Participate in delegating duties, organizing, planning, making decisions, and taking action in group setting.
Participate in persuading, compromising, debating, and negotiating in the resolution of conflicts and differences.

C. SOCIAL AND POLITICAL PARTICIPATION SKILLS

Keep informed on issues that affect society.
Identify situation in which social action is required.
Work individually or with others to decide on an appropriate course of action.
Work to influence those in positions of social power to strive for extensions of freedom, social justice, and human rights.
Accept and fulfill social responsibilities associated with citizenship in a free society.

(Reprinted with permission from National Council for the Social Studies, *Expectations of Excellence*, pp. 148–149.)

Appendix B
The Essential Social Studies Skills Checklist

The Essential Social Studies Skills Checklist

It can be very easy to overlook or lose track of the skills portion of social studies because there is so much content to teach. Skill building is a major component of the social studies, precisely because of its overwhelming content load; there is no way to cover it all. We can help our students to develop the skills they need in order to direct their own learning.

This simple chart allows you to keep track of the skills you are teaching your students. You list the skills you want the students to master in the first column, then simply make a check when you have introduced the skill, another check when you have given the students a chance to practice it (more than once), and a third when they have mastered it. You can make the chart more complicated, specifying what each entry means (what it means to master a certain skill), but simple is good.

Skill	I	P	M

Best Practices in Social Studies

1. In-depth study rather than cursory coverage is encouraged.
2. Activities that involve student inquiry and problem solving about significant issues rather than memorization of isolated facts are desirable.
3. Interactive, cooperative group study is stronger than lecture style or round-robin reading processes.
4. Integration with other curriculum areas is highly recommended.
5. Rich content should begin in elementary school.
6. Study of diversity and multiple points of view rather than a single, dominant cultural heritage is essential.
7. Promotion of students' sense of ownership in the social studies curriculum by allowing student choices and discoveries is paramount.
8. Use of evaluation that involves further learning and open

expression of ideas should prevail over the unit test of factual knowledge or textbook information.

9. Learning should be fun.
10. Students should feel the teacher's unconditional acceptance.
11. Teachers should remove all threat from the classroom.

(Adapted from *Best Practices: New Standards for Teaching and Learning in America's Schools*, 2nd edition.)

Appendix C
Window on the World Checklist

Window on the World Checklist

Name _____

Check one:

Country in Asia (4th and 5th)   Name of Country _____

Country in Europe (4th and 5th)   Name of Country _____

Country in North America/Caribbean   Name of Country _____

State in North America (5th only)   Name of State _____

Country in South America (4th only)   Name of Country _____

1. Map (30 points)
   Reasonably accurate?
   Informative?
   Clearly a physical, political, or product/pictorial map?
   Has a legend?
   Has a compass rose?
   Names the country?   Points _____

2. Inside Features (60 points)
   Has at least three clear sections that inform and interest the reader?
   Choose from the following or check with me:

comics	recipes	fast facts
animals	buildings	photos/postcards
menu	folktale	visitor's log or diary
daily life	environment	special products

   Things you might want to buy.
   Places you might want to visit.
   Famous people from this country.   Points _____

3. Cover/Author (10 points)
   Attractive?
   Thoughtful?
   Book turned in on due date?
   About the Author on the back cover?   Points _____

   Total Points _____

   Comments:

Appendix D
Immigrant Biography

Immigrant Biography

Character Name_____Students_____

Age _____ Height _____ Weight _____

Country of birth _____ Urban or rural _____

Birth family _____

Childhood memories _____

Favorite foods from original country _____

Favorite games or hobbies (in original country) _____

Parent's work _____

When did your character come to the U.S.?_____

Why did they choose to come?_____

How did they decide to come Seattle? _____

What did they leave behind? _____

How did they get to Seattle?_____

Did they stop anywhere on the way?_____

How long have they been in Seattle?_____

What do they miss most about their homeland? _____

What do they like most about being in Seattle?_____

Current family? _____

Pets _____

Current job or situation _____

Hopes _____

Fears _____

Appendix E
The Model House Project

The Model House Project

The major part of this assignment is for you to construct a model of the building in which your character lived before he or she left for the United States. This structure should be accurate in its basic shape and design. Make sure that your model is round if most of the houses in your character's hometown, city, or village were round. Make it look like it is made out of wood if the homes were made from wood. Make it look like it is made of bricks if the houses of that place are mostly made from bricks. You don't have to use the actual materials to make this model. You should find materials that are easy and safe to work with. You should also find materials that are cheap to work with. Cereal boxes are a good building material for this project. The boxes are easy to cut and to shape, and they hold together with tape.

You are making a model of a house or building. It should be large enough to be easily seen. It should be light enough and small enough for you to carry it to school and back home. We will be displaying our models for others to see, so do your best work.

We have gathered some books about the countries in which your characters used to live. These books will help you to find the information you need to build the model and to answer the questions.

You are also encouraged to get information from your own sources. You can talk with people who used to live in the country you are researching. You may use the internet if you have access to that, or anything else that will help you to create the model.

This project is due on _____. You will have some time during class to work on it, but you will also have to find time to work on this project outside of school.

Appendix F
Housing Project

Housing Project

These questions will help you on your way to creating a model of your character's house in his or her country of origin (the place he or she lived before coming to the United States).

Your character's name_____ Student name _____

1. What country is your character from?

2. What is the average temperature in this country?

3. How hot does it get during the hottest time of year? When is this time?

4. How cold does it get during the coldest time of year? When is this time (what months)?

5. How much rain or snow does your country get? Is it spread out through the year or are there periods when it is very wet and periods when it is very dry?

6. What is the land like where your character lived? Is it in the mountains, near a river, near a desert, in the jungle or a forest? Is it a large city that used to be filled with trees or used to be a desert?

7. Did your character live near many people or in a small town or village?

8. What were the houses made out of in this place?

9. Did those materials come from near the house or did they come from somewhere else?

10. Who built the house? Was it the people who lived in it or was it someone they hired?

11. How long did it take to build the house?

12. How long do they expect the house to last?

13. Who lived in the house? Was it one family, or one extended family (lots of cousins and aunts and uncles and grandparents)? Or many different family together?

14. Is there anything else we should know about this place where your character lived?

Appendix G
Reflection on Model Project

Reflection on Model Project

1. What did I enjoy most about the project?
2. What was the most challenging thing about it?
3. What did I do that was most helpful?
4. What would I do differently next time?
5. What do I think was the best thing about my work?
6. What did I learn from this project?